One-Pot Cookies

BROADWAY BOOKS · NEW YORK

One-Pot Cookies

**60 Recipes for Making
Cookies from Scratch,
Using a Pot, a Spoon,
and a Pan**

Andrew Schloss

with Ken Bookman

BROADWAY

ONE-POT COOKIES. Copyright © 1998 by Andrew Schloss with Ken Bookman. All rights reserved. Printed in the United States of America. No part of this book may be reproduced or transmitted in any form or by any means, electronic or mechanical, including photocopying, recording, or by any information storage and retrieval system, without written permission from the publisher. For information, address Broadway Books, a division of Bantam Doubleday Dell Publishing Group, Inc., 1540 Broadway, New York, NY 10036.

Broadway Books titles may be purchased for business or promotional use or for special sales. For information, please write to: Special Markets Department, Bantam Doubleday Dell Publishing Group, Inc., 1540 Broadway, New York, NY 10036.

BROADWAY BOOKS and its logo, a letter B bisected on the diagonal, are trademarks of Broadway Books, a division of Bantam Doubleday Dell Publishing Group, Inc.

Library of Congress Cataloging-in-Publication Data
Schloss, Andrew, 1951–
    One-pot cookies : 60 recipes for making cookies from scratch, using a
pot, a spoon, and a pan / Andrew Schloss with Ken Bookman. — 1st ed.
      p.   cm.
    Includes index.
    ISBN 0-7679-0122-3
    1. Cookies   2. Desserts.   3. Quick and easy cookery.   I. Bookman,
Ken. II. Title.
    TX772.S345   1998
    641.8′654—dc21   97-31346
                                                        CIP

FIRST EDITION

Designed by Debbie Glasserman

98 99 00 01 02 10 9 8 7 6 5 4 3 2 1

To our readers, with thanks.

Contents

Acknowledgments

Our sincere thanks to everyone who made this book possible—our agent, Judith Weber; our editor at Broadway Books, Harriet Bell; our copyeditor, Angela Renkowski; and the designer of these pages, Debbie Glasserman. Our gratitude also to our families and friends for their critiques and their support.

Introduction

feel like a charlatan. *One-Pot Cookies?* Who am I kidding? Cookies that take more than one container for mixing are almost unheard of. But the bother with cookies isn't in the mixing; it's in the baking. Batch after batch—each one a test to see whether it will be the one that scorches, sticks, or refuses to brown.

Well, it's not completely dishonest to apply the one-pot method to cookie-baking. Every recipe in this book follows the same one-pot precept of all our one-pot dessert books: a single pot for mixing, a single spoon for mixing, and a single pan for baking. All the recipes take only ten minutes to assemble, and none requires more than a few minutes of cleanup. The difference here happens in the oven. By turning recipes into bar cookies, I've made sure there are no more batches, no more burning, no more tests. And all your favorites are here: brownies, oatmeal cookies, shortbreads, fruit-filled cookies, nut clusters, chocolate cookies, macaroons, and biscotti.

In perfecting these recipes, I've developed some unusual techniques. I have learned to trim the preparation and baking time for biscotti from three hours to less than one. I have created one-pot cookies that are multilayered, multicolored, and exotically flavored. I have worked with ingredients I never thought could go into a cookie, such as rosemary in the fragrant Orange Rosemary Shortbread on page 61, biscotti that use coffee grounds (page 15), and a whole-grain cookie made with tabbouleh (page 53). There's also a recipe for home-made graham crackers that will redefine the commercial standard you have grown used to. There are perfumed, Indian-inspired shortbreads, wheat germ brownies that taste as if they were made with butterscotch, and a pecan pie turned into a delicate chewy morsel.

I've had fun, and although most of the recipes have taken numerous tries and multiple batches, I've burned my cookies so you don't have to burn yours.

How to Use This Book

If you're familiar with the first one-pot dessert book, *One-Pot Cakes,* you know how it streamlined the traditional method of making a cake into something so simple it could be an everyday, spur-of-the-moment activity.

One-Pot Cookies applies the same principles to cookies, shortbreads, biscotti, and brownies.

To review those principles:

- The creaming of butter and sugar is simplified by melting the butter and stirring in the sugar along with the other ingredients.
- Sifting dry ingredients has been eliminated. There's only one reason to sift flour, and that's to aerate it. The notion that sifting dry ingredients mixes them is false. Contrary to popular opinion, the dry ingredients don't combine until the batter is stirred.
- When chocolate is part of the recipe, it is added to the butter, where it can melt without danger of scorching.
- Less heat-sensitive ingredients—sugar, vanilla, and spices—are added even before the

eggs go in. The eggs are added after the mixture cools to prevent curdling, then the dry ingredients are added.

- Baking powder and baking soda are added in pinches to eliminate lumps before they go into the batter and so they can soften and disperse evenly through the liquid before more dry ingredients are added.

In short, the one-pot method gives you the quality of a baked good made from scratch with the convenience of a mix—and with less cleanup.

About the Ingredients

Brown sugar. Brown sugar is granulated sugar with molasses added. Dark brown sugar has more molasses; light has less. Because brown sugar is prone to lumping, you should pack it into the measuring cup to get an accurate measure.

Butter. I use only unsalted butter. The salt content among different brands of salted butter varies so greatly it's impossible to predict the flavor of a baked good in which salted butter is used.

Chocolate. The recipes in this book were tested with Baker's, Nestlé, and Hershey's chocolates—the most commonly available brands. I have used them interchangeably for many years with consistently excellent results. White chocolate is not chocolate at all. What we buy as white chocolate is nothing more than sweet, vanilla-flavored fat. However, because it is an emulsion, white chocolate, like other chocolates, has the same sensitivities to moisture and heat.

Cocoa. Cocoa powder is unsweetened chocolate that has about 75 percent of its fat removed. European cocoas are Dutch-processed, which means the chocolate is treated with a mild alkaline, and it is milder, darker, and more easily mixed in liquid. Either type can be used when cocoa powder is called for.

Coffee. When a dessert calls for instant-coffee powder, use any brand. Freeze-dried coffee also is fine. There is one recipe, Walnut Coffee Dunkers (page 15), that calls for finely ground dark-roast coffee. Use unbrewed noninstant ground coffee beans.

Cornmeal. I use yellow or white cornmeal. As with flours, store cornmeal in your freezer to keep it fresh.

Dried citrus peel. Minced dried lemon and orange peels are sold in the spice section of many supermarkets or in specialty stores. Using them will save you labor and cleanup. Freshly grated or minced citrus zest can be substituted for the dried product without adjusting the measurement.

Dried fruit. Several recipes call for dried fruit, including raisins (both golden and dark), currants, cherries, cranberries (sold under the brand name Craisins), and blueberries. The only ones that might not be available at your supermarket are dried cherries and blueberries; these are available in gourmet food stores and many health-food stores, and they are worth seeking out. Look for dried sour (or red) cherries for the best flavor.

Eggs. The desserts were tested with large and extra-large eggs; either size is fine.

Flour. Unbleached all-purpose flour was used in testing; either bleached or unbleached works fine. Some of the shortbreads call for cake flour. Do *not* use self-rising cake flour. The whole wheat flour used in testing was regular grind. You do *not* need whole wheat pastry flour.

Milk. Use any milk you have on hand. Fat content will not affect these recipes.

Nuts. I have used a wide range of nuts and seeds in these recipes. Most are available in supermarkets, but some, such as sunflower seeds, pumpkin seeds, and pine nuts, might have to come from a specialty store. When a ground nut is specified, I have used only varieties that are available already ground so you can avoid using another piece of kitchen equipment. However, for a fresher product, and if you don't mind the little extra time and cleanup of grinding them yourself, use whole nuts and grind them in a food processor or mini-chopper (see Grinding nuts, page 4).

Spray shortening. These sprays (Pam is a common brand) make a two-second task out of greasing a baking pan with vegetable shortening.

About the Techniques

Grinding nuts. I call for preground nuts to help minimize cleanup, but if you have a food processor or mini-chopper and an extra minute or two, grinding nuts yourself makes a fresher product. Measure about 25 percent more nut pieces than the volume of ground nuts the recipe calls for (if using a weight measure, the measurement stays the same). Use the pulse button of your processor in two or three bursts of no more than 5 seconds' duration to coarsely chop the nuts. Continue pulsing in shorter bursts until the nuts are uniformly ground into a powder as fine as sand. The goal is to get the nuts as fine as possible without transforming them into nut butter. If they begin to clump or look oily, stop and use them as they are.

Melting butter and chocolate. In recipes that call for melting butter and/or chocolate, use a 3-quart, heavy-bottomed saucepan for mixing the batter. When a recipe calls for melted chocolate, begin melting butter over medium heat first. Use your hands to break the chocolate into pieces and add the pieces after the butter has melted about halfway. The melted butter protects the chocolate from scorching, so you can keep the chocolate over the heat until it is about half melted. Then remove the mixture from the heat and allow the residual heat to finish the melting.

Moistening hands. When a cookie dough is thick, the easiest way to spread it evenly across the bottom of a pan is to press it into place with your fingers. This can be messy unless you moisten your hands first. Because the main fluid in most cookie batters and doughs is fat, and because fat is repelled by water, you can keep the batter or dough from sticking to your fingers by moistening them with cold tap water. Shake off excess water so your fingers aren't *too* wet or you will water down the batter or dough. If the batter or dough starts to stick, remoisten your hands and continue pressing.

Pinching in baking powder and soda. To avoid lumps, measure baking powder and soda into your hand and pinch them in with your fingers. Stir well until dissolved. Add baking powder and soda to the batter before the flour. Stir well, but don't concern yourself with a few streaks. These will disappear when you stir in the flour.

About the Baking Pans

In recipes that call for melting butter and/or chocolate, use a 3-quart, heavy-bottomed saucepan for mixing the batter. It doesn't matter what type of metal the saucepan is made of. In recipes that don't require melting, use that same saucepan or a large mixing bowl.

Although the types of cookies in this book vary widely, I've limited baking pans to those found in a typical home kitchen:

- 8- and 9-inch square baking pans
- 9 × 13 × 2-inch baking pan
- 10 × 15 × 1-inch jellyroll pan
- 12-cup standard muffin tin
- 9-inch pie plate

One of the most talked-about variables in baking is the color of the pan. I don't consider it as crucial as you may have been led to believe. Both glass and dark-colored metal absorb heat faster than shiny metal pans. Far more important than the color of the pan are your oven's temperature and the likelihood that it has some hot and cold spots. If you've noticed that some of your baking pans transfer heat faster than others, lower your oven heat by 25 degrees when you use those pans.

Cookies that have a tendency to stick, such as macaroons and brownies, benefit from lining the pan with waxed paper or foil.

To remove the baked cookie from the pan, allow it to cool in the pan for about 15 minutes. In that time, the cookie will harden slightly. Run a small, sharp knife around the edge of the layer to loosen it. Then cut the layer into bars and remove them from the pan with a small spatula. Cool the rest of the way on a rack.

Dunking Cookies

Biscotti are anti-cookies.

They're brittle, dry, and hardly sweet, lacking in every sensuous quality we've come to expect from a cookie. And yet we love them. And why not? They're guiltless. Compared to the fat, cloying joys of a gooey chocolate chip or a double-cream sandwich cookie, the subtlety of biscotti seems downright righteous, challenging us to savor the butter in a toasted nut, the natural sugar in a dried currant, and the decadent delight of dunking.

Biscotti beg for a dive into a cup of black coffee or milky tea. Absent a liquid partner, many just aren't worth the effort. They are simply too hard, too Spartanly sugarless, to be eaten alone.

There is no reasonable explanation for this. Biscotti shouldn't have to shatter teeth to be authentic. Dunking them should be an opportunity, not a requirement. To that end, I have created biscotti that are crisp without being hard and that can be baked in a fraction of the time.

Usually, biscotti dough is formed into a loaf and refrigerated for several hours to firm. It is then baked twice (the literal meaning of "biscotti"): first for an hour as a loaf, then in slices for another hour to ensure cookies that are cooked through and crisp.

One-Pot Cookies

One-pot biscotti dough is mixed up in a saucepan, as are all one-pot recipes, and baked in a single flat layer in a square baking pan for only 20 minutes. The baked layer is then cut into rectangular slices that are crisped in the oven for 25 minutes. This reduces the traditional baking time from 3 hours to 45 minutes.

To be sure, biscotti aren't the only cookies that cry out for dunking. Any plain, firm, or semifirm biscuit can benefit from a quick dip in a flavorful liquid. In this chapter, you will find sugar cookies, gingersnaps, butter cookies, and macaroons, as well as biscotti, rusks, zwieback, and kamish bread—all different names to describe the same kind of bar cookie that is baked twice to help it dry, crisp, toast, and prepare itself for a bracing dunk.

Fragrant Sugar Cookies

In this cookie, cardamom, a floral gingerlike spice familiar to most as the fragrance of Swedish coffee cake, is teamed with lemon in a crisp, cakey biscuit that goes perfectly with herb teas. Store these cookies in a tightly closed jar, and they will keep for a week or more.

MAKES 4 DOZEN COOKIES

¼ **pound (1 stick) unsalted butter**
1 teaspoon dried lemon peel
½ **teaspoon ground cardamom**
¾ **cup plus 2 tablespoons sugar**
¼ **teaspoon salt**

¼ **cup milk**
1 teaspoon vanilla extract
1 egg
1 teaspoon baking powder
1½ **cups flour**

Preheat oven to 375°F. Coat a 10 × 15 × 1-inch jellyroll pan with spray shortening.

In a large, heavy-bottomed saucepan over medium heat, melt the butter. Stir in the lemon peel, cardamom, ¾ cup of sugar, salt, milk, vanilla, and egg until well mixed. Add the baking powder in pinches to break up any lumps and stir until batter is smooth. Stir in the flour and beat well.

Pour and scrape the batter into the prepared pan. Moisten your hands and shake off excess water. Gently press the batter into an even layer with your fingertips, remoistening your fingers if they start to stick to the batter. Sprinkle the remaining 2 tablespoons of sugar evenly over the top.

Bake for 12 to 15 minutes, until the edges are browned and the center is firm. Remove from the oven and cool on a rack for 10 minutes. Cut into 48 squares or diamonds by cutting on the diagonal.

One-Pot Cookies

Fire-Tongue Ginger Biscuits

These moist, mahogany biscuits are not for the faint-of-palate. They flare with cinnamon, ginger, coffee, and an afterglow of black pepper. The biscuits vary in texture. Those cut from the edge will be snapping crisp; those taken from the center will be softer and more cakelike. You can alter the texture with the size of the baking pan: A smaller pan will yield softer, thicker cookies; a larger one, thinner and crisper cookies.

Makes 4 dozen cookies

1/4 **pound (1 stick) unsalted butter**	3/4 **cup dark brown sugar**
2 **teaspoons ground ginger**	1/4 **cup strong coffee**
1/8 **teaspoon allspice**	1 **egg**
1/2 **teaspoon ground black pepper**	1/2 **teaspoon baking soda**
1/2 **teaspoon ground cinnamon**	11/2 **cups flour**
1 **tablespoon cocoa powder**	2 **tablespoons granulated sugar**

Preheat oven to 375°F. Coat a 10 × 15 × 1-inch jellyroll pan with spray shortening.

In a large, heavy-bottomed saucepan over medium heat, melt the butter. Remove from heat. Stir in the ginger, allspice, pepper, cinnamon, cocoa, brown sugar, coffee, and egg. Mix well. Add the baking soda in pinches to break up any lumps and stir until batter is smooth. Stir in the flour and beat well.

Pour and scrape the batter into the prepared pan. Moisten your hands and shake off excess water. Gently press the batter into an even layer with your fingertips, remoistening your fingers if they start to stick to the batter. Sprinkle the granulated sugar evenly over the top.

Bake for 12 to 15 minutes, until the edges are browned and the center is firm. Remove from the oven and cool on a rack for 10 minutes. Cut into 48 squares or diamonds by cutting on the diagonal.

Hazelnut Crunch

A cross between butter-crunch candy and shortbread, these cookies benefit from the increased presence of toasted ground hazelnuts. If you can't find them at your local market, grind your own hazelnuts as described on page 4 and toast them with the melting butter. You also can substitute another ground nut.

MAKES 25 COOKIES

$^1/_4$ **pound (1 stick) unsalted butter**
$^1/_2$ **cup confectioners' sugar**
$^1/_2$ **cup granulated sugar**
$^1/_8$ **teaspoon almond extract**
1 teaspoon vanilla extract

1 egg
Pinch of salt
1$^1/_2$ cups flour
1 cup ground hazelnuts

Preheat oven to 350°F. Coat a 9-inch square baking pan with spray shortening.

In a large, heavy-bottomed saucepan over medium heat, melt the butter. Remove pan from heat and stir in the sugars, extracts, egg, and salt until smooth. Stir in the flour and hazelnuts until ingredients are well combined.

Pour and scrape the batter into the prepared pan. Moisten your hands and shake off excess water. Gently press the batter into an even layer with your fingertips, remoistening your fingers if they start to stick to the batter.

Bake for 25 minutes, until the edges are golden brown and the cookie is just set. Remove pan from the oven and cool on a rack for 5 minutes. Cut into 25 squares and cool for at least 15 minutes more.

Orange-Pecan Ginger Toasts

These orange-scented praline biscotti are inspired by New Orleans. The flavors are rich and aromatic, the tint mocha, the texture crisp but yielding. These biscotti are particularly excellent dunked into espresso or a milk-laced cup of strong orange-spice tea.

MAKES 16 COOKIES

4 tablespoons ($^1/_2$ stick) unsalted butter
2 cups pecan halves
1 tablespoon dried orange peel
$^3/_4$ cup light brown sugar
1 teaspoon ground ginger
$^1/_2$ teaspoon vanilla extract

$^1/_4$ teaspoon orange extract
$^1/_4$ teaspoon salt
2 eggs
$^1/_4$ teaspoon baking powder
$^3/_4$ cup plus 1 tablespoon flour

Preheat oven to 350°F. Coat a 9-inch square baking pan with spray shortening.

In a large, heavy-bottomed saucepan over medium heat, melt the butter. Add the pecan halves and cook until nuts are lightly toasted. Remove from heat and mix in the orange peel, sugar, ginger, extracts, and salt, and mix until thoroughly blended. Beat in the eggs. Add the baking powder in pinches to break up any lumps and stir thoroughly. Stir in the flour until a smooth dough forms.

Place the dough in the prepared pan. Moisten your hands and shake off excess water. Gently press the dough into an even layer with your fingertips, remoistening your fingers if they start to stick to the dough.

Bake for 20 minutes and remove the pan from the oven. Cover with a cutting board and invert pan. Remove the pan. Cut in half with a serrated knife and cut each half into 8 rectangular strips. Place the strips back in the pan, setting each on a narrow side. Return pan to the oven to bake for 25 more minutes, until golden brown and crisp.

Chocolate Chip Zwieback

These crispy rusk cookies (rusk is the English version of biscotti) are loaded with specks of choco-late and crumbled, toasted nuts, which keep them from becoming too hard. Rather, the cookies crunch at first bite, then cascade into a jumble of melt-in-your-mouth crumbs.

MAKES 16 COOKIES

1 cup semisweet mini–chocolate chips
4 tablespoons ($^1/_2$ stick) unsalted butter
$^1/_2$ cup finely ground almonds, walnuts, or
   hazelnuts
$^3/_4$ cup sugar
1 teaspoon vanilla extract

$^1/_4$ teaspoon almond extract
$^1/_4$ teaspoon salt
2 eggs
$^1/_4$ teaspoon baking powder
1 cup flour

Place chips in the freezer. Preheat oven to 350°F. Line a 9-inch square baking pan with foil and coat with spray shortening.

In a large, heavy-bottomed saucepan over medium heat, begin melting the butter. When it is half melted, remove from heat and stir until butter is completely melted. Mix in the nuts, sugar, extracts, and salt until ingredients are thoroughly combined. Beat in the eggs. Add the baking powder in pinches to break up any lumps and stir thoroughly. Stir in the flour until a smooth dough forms. Remove chocolate chips from freezer and mix into dough.

Place the dough in the prepared pan. Moisten your hands and shake off excess water. Gently press the dough into an even layer with your fingertips, remoistening your fingers if they start to stick to the dough.

Bake for 20 minutes and remove the pan from the oven. Cover with a cutting board and invert pan. Remove the pan and the foil. Cut in half with a serrated knife and cut each half into 8 rectangular strips. Place the strips back in the pan, setting each on a narrow side. Return pan to the oven to bake for 25 more minutes, until golden brown and crisp.

Pignoli Lemon Biscotti

Pine nuts are one of the few nuts and seeds that remain strictly savory in the minds of most cooks. We grind them into pesto and toss them over sautés, but we almost never bake with them. In this cookie, however, pine nuts are toasted in melted butter and accented with a hint of dried lemon peel. What emerges is a florally fragrant biscuit, crisp and rich with nuts.

MAKES 16 COOKIES

4 tablespoons ($^1/_2$ stick) unsalted butter
$1^1/_2$ cups pine nuts
2 tablespoons dried lemon peel
$^3/_4$ cup sugar
$^1/_4$ teaspoon ground cardamom

1 teaspoon vanilla extract
$^1/_8$ teaspoon salt
2 eggs
$^1/_4$ teaspoon baking powder
1 cup flour

Preheat oven to 350°F. Coat a 9-inch square baking pan with spray shortening.

In a large, heavy-bottomed saucepan over medium heat, melt the butter. Add the pine nuts and cook until nuts are lightly toasted. Remove from heat and add the lemon peel, sugar, cardamom, vanilla, and salt. Mix until ingredients are thoroughly blended. Beat in the eggs. Add the baking powder in pinches to break up any lumps and stir thoroughly. Stir in the flour until a smooth dough forms.

Place the dough in the prepared pan. Moisten your hands and shake off excess water. Gently press the dough into an even layer with your fingertips, remoistening your fingers if they start to stick to the dough.

Bake for 20 minutes and remove the pan from the oven. Cover with a cutting board and invert pan. Remove the pan. Cut in half with a serrated knife and cut each half into 8 rectangular strips. Place the strips back in the pan, setting each on a narrow side. Return to the oven to bake for 25 more minutes, until golden brown and crisp.

Sesame Butter Bricks

Reminiscent of Italian sesame biscuits, these shortbreadlike cookies are inundated with toasted sesame seeds. They are decidedly adult, not too sweet, and excessively rich.

MAKES 28 COOKIES

$^1/_4$ **pound (1 stick) unsalted butter**
1 cup toasted sesame seeds
$^1/_2$ **cup confectioners' sugar**
$^1/_2$ **cup granulated sugar**
1 teaspoon vanilla extract

1 egg
Pinch of salt
1 teaspoon baking powder
1$^3/_4$ cups all-purpose flour
$^1/_2$ **cup whole wheat flour**

Preheat oven to 350°F. Coat a 9 × 13 × 2-inch baking pan with spray shortening.

In a large, heavy-bottomed saucepan over medium heat, begin melting the butter. When it is half melted, add the sesame seeds and cook until the butter is completely melted, stirring often. Remove from the heat and stir in the sugars, vanilla, egg, and salt until smooth.

Add the baking powder in pinches to break up any lumps and stir thoroughly. Stir in the all-purpose and whole wheat flours until well combined.

Pour and scrape the batter into the prepared pan. Moisten your hands and shake off excess water. Gently press the batter into an even layer with your fingertips, remoistening your fingers if they start to stick to the batter.

Bake for 20 minutes, until the edges are golden brown and the cookie is just set. Remove from the oven and cool on a rack for at least 15 minutes. Cut into 28 squares.

Walnut Coffee Dunkers

The surprise in these cookies is the peppering of ground coffee that permeates the dough. The bursts of coffee flavor are underscored by toasted walnuts and the richness of browned butter.

MAKES 16 COOKIES

4 tablespoons ($^1/_2$ stick) unsalted butter

2 cups walnut pieces

2 tablespoons finely ground dark-roast coffee (noninstant)

$^3/_4$ cup sugar

1 teaspoon vanilla extract

$^1/_4$ teaspoon almond extract

$^1/_8$ teaspoon salt

2 eggs

$^1/_4$ teaspoon baking powder

1 cup flour

Preheat oven to 350°F. Coat a 9-inch square baking pan with spray shortening.

In a large, heavy-bottomed saucepan over medium heat, melt the butter. Add the walnuts and cook until lightly toasted. Remove from heat and mix in the ground coffee, sugar, extracts, and salt. Mix until thoroughly blended. Beat in the eggs. Add the baking powder in pinches to break up any lumps and stir thoroughly. Stir in the flour until a smooth dough forms.

Place the dough in the prepared pan. Moisten your hands and shake off excess water. Gently press the dough into an even layer with your fingertips, remoistening your fingers if they start to stick to the dough.

Bake for 20 minutes and remove the pan from the oven. Cover with a cutting board and invert pan. Remove the pan. Cut in half with a serrated knife and cut each half into 8 rectangular strips. Place the strips back in the pan, setting each on a narrow side. Return pan to the oven to bake for 25 more minutes, until golden brown and crisp.

Chocolate Kamish Bread

Kamish bread is the Jewish version of biscotti. This recipe has the novel addition of cornmeal toasted in the melted butter. The toasting gives the chocolate a dark-roast flavor, and the cornmeal keeps the cookies from becoming too hard.

MAKES 20 COOKIES

4 tablespoons ($^1/_2$ stick) unsalted butter
$^1/_3$ cup cornmeal
2 ounces unsweetened chocolate, broken
  in pieces
I cup sugar
I teaspoon vanilla extract

$^1/_4$ teaspoon salt
2 eggs
$^1/_4$ teaspoon baking powder
I cup flour
I cup semisweet mini–chocolate chips

Preheat oven to 350°F. Line a 9-inch square baking pan with foil and coat with spray shortening.

In a large, heavy-bottomed saucepan over medium heat, melt the butter. Add the cornmeal and continue cooking, stirring constantly, until the cornmeal begins to toast lightly. Remove from heat. Add the chocolate and stir until melted.

Mix in the sugar, vanilla, and salt until thoroughly combined. Beat in the eggs. Add the baking powder in pinches to break up any lumps and stir thoroughly. Stir in the flour until a smooth dough forms. Stir in the chocolate chips.

Pour and scrape the dough into the prepared pan. Moisten your hands and shake off excess water. Gently press the dough into an even layer with your fingertips, remoistening your fingers if they start to stick to the dough.

Bake for 20 minutes and remove the pan from the oven. Cover with a cutting board and invert pan. Remove the pan and the foil. Cut in half with a serrated knife and cut each half into 10 rectangular strips. Place the strips back in the pan, setting each on a narrow side. Return to the oven to bake for 25 more minutes, until crisp.

One-Pot Cookies

Seedy Biscotti

These cookies, perfect for dunking, are loaded with seeds and nuts, which can be used in just about any combination. The seeds go well with the spices that form the aromatic foundation for these elegant biscotti.

MAKES 20 COOKIES

4 tablespoons ($^1/_2$ stick) unsalted butter
2 cups assorted seeds and/or nuts
   (sunflower seeds, pumpkin seeds, pine
   nuts, sesame seeds, poppy seeds, etc.)
1 cup sugar
1 teaspoon ground cinnamon

$^1/_8$ teaspoon ground allspice
1 teaspoon vanilla extract
Pinch of salt
2 eggs
$^1/_4$ teaspoon baking powder
$^3/_4$ cup whole wheat flour

Preheat oven to 350°F. Coat a 9-inch square baking pan with spray shortening.

In a large, heavy-bottomed saucepan over medium heat, melt the butter. Add the seeds and nuts and cook until they are lightly toasted. Remove from heat and mix in the sugar, cinnamon, allspice, vanilla, and salt. Blend thoroughly. Beat in the eggs. Add the baking powder in pinches to break up any lumps and stir thoroughly. Stir in the flour until a smooth dough forms.

Place the dough in the prepared pan. Moisten your hands and shake off excess water. Gently press the dough into an even layer with your fingertips, remoistening your fingers if they start to stick to the dough.

Bake for 20 minutes and remove the pan from the oven. Cover with a cutting board and invert pan. Remove the pan. Cut in half with a serrated knife and cut each half into 10 strips. Place the strips back in the pan, setting each on a narrow side. Return pan to the oven to bake for 25 more minutes, until golden brown and crisp.

Chocolate Cookies

Before there were mocha almond tortes, chocolate silk pies, and chocolate Grand Marnier mousses, there was just a chocolate cookie, a glass of milk, and you.

Chocolate cookies are at once the most seductive and most innocent of indulgences. From wafer-plain to brownie-rich, they have the power to turn a cup of tea into an instant luxury or end an opulent meal with welcome simplicity. They can be chockful of chocolate, clustered with nuts, or filled with dried fruit. There are chocolate macaroons, chocolate sugar cookies, gooey chocolate bars, classic chocolate chip cookies, and buttery chocolate shortbreads. The best part is that all these chocolate cookies are in this book, and every one of them can be made in one pot.

The same chocolate assets and pitfalls I spoke of in the companion book, *One-Pot Chocolate Desserts,* apply here. The assets are obvious to anyone who has ever bitten into a chocolate chip. I'll review the pitfalls briefly.

Chocolate burns easily, which is why most cookbooks warn against melting chocolate without the protection of a double boiler or a cautiously programmed microwave. The one-pot method eliminates the need for a double boiler. In these recipes, bar chocolate is added to hot melted butter, melted partially over heat, then removed and stirred until the residual heat melts the remaining chocolate. This method not only protects against burning but also cools the butter to keep it from damaging other heat-sensitive ingredients, such as eggs.

Also, melted chocolate can separate when it is mixed with liquids. But by mixing it with butter, this tendency is greatly reduced.

I used unsweetened and semisweet bar chocolates and chocolate chips and chunks and cocoa powder in developing these recipes. The brands were Nestlé, Hershey's, and Baker's, used interchangeably with consistently excellent results. In my opinion, fine, expensive chocolates are wasted in cookie recipes. Save them (and your money) for desserts in which the quality of the chocolate is paramount.

The principal difference among unsweetened, semisweet, and bittersweet chocolates is their level of sweetening. Sweetening is a matter of how much sugar and cocoa solids the chocolate contains. Generally speaking, the sweeter a chocolate, the less intensely chocolate it is. That's why it is tricky to substitute one type of chocolate for another. The difference will not be just a question of sweetness; the entire flavor profile will change.

Chocolate Cherry Bars

This is a soft brownie, rocky with gobs of dried sour cherry, perched on a shingle of the palest, thinnest, most buttery of pastries. Its construction appears far too complex to have come from a single vessel, and its flavor is just as multidimensional.

MAKES 3 DOZEN COOKIES

12 tablespoons (1½ sticks) unsalted
  butter
⅓ cup granulated sugar
1½ cups flour
¾ cup dark brown sugar
2 tablespoons cocoa powder (preferably
  Dutch-processed)

3 eggs
1 teaspoon vanilla extract
1 cup ground hazelnuts or almonds
1 cup dried sour (or red) cherries

Preheat oven to 350°F. Coat a 9-inch square baking pan with spray shortening.

In a large, heavy-bottomed saucepan over medium heat, melt the butter. Stir in the granulated sugar and flour to form a smooth, thick dough.

Place all but 3 to 4 tablespoons of this mixture in the prepared pan. Moisten your hands and shake off excess water. Gently press the dough into an even layer with your fingertips, remoistening your fingers if they start to stick to the dough. Bake for 10 minutes, until pale golden.

Meanwhile, add the brown sugar and cocoa to the dough remaining in the saucepan. Mix well. Mix in the eggs, vanilla, nuts, and cherries. Pour into the baking pan over the layer of baked pastry and smooth into an even layer.

Return pan to the oven and bake for 20 more minutes. Cool on a rack for at least 15 minutes. Slice into 36 squares and remove with a small spatula.

Mud Pies

I have rarely met a cookie that was better than its batter. So I strive, whenever appropriate, for a consistency wet enough to remind me of batter but firm enough to pass for a cookie. This fudgy puddle of a cookie, erupting with nuts and mega-chocolate chunks, does just that.

MAKES 25 COOKIES

6 tablespoons (³/₄ stick) unsalted butter
8 ounces semisweet chocolate, broken in pieces
1 tablespoon instant coffee powder
³/₄ cup sugar
Pinch of salt
2 eggs

2 teaspoons vanilla extract
1 teaspoon baking powder
¹/₃ cup flour
1 cup nuts (pistachios, walnut or pecan pieces, chopped almonds, etc.)
1 package (about 12 ounces) chocolate chunks, or mega-morsels

Preheat oven to 325°F. Coat a 9-inch square baking pan with spray shortening and dust with flour.

In a large, heavy-bottomed saucepan over medium heat, begin melting the butter. When it is half melted, add the chocolate. Remove from the heat when the chocolate is half melted and stir until the butter and chocolate are completely melted. Stir in the coffee powder, sugar, salt, eggs, and vanilla. Add the baking powder in pinches to break up any lumps. Then stir in the flour, nuts, and chocolate chunks.

Pour and scrape the batter into the prepared pan and smooth into an even layer. Bake for 25 minutes, until the top is crusty but still soft inside. Remove from the oven and cool on a rack to room temperature. Cut into 25 squares.

Chocolate Tea Biscuits

These cookies are plain chocolate, altered by an afterthought of almond. Short and not too sweet, they are just the thing to accompany a cup of tea and a handful of ripe berries.

MAKES 25 COOKIES

¹/₄ **pound (I stick) unsalted butter**
¹/₄ **cup ground almonds**
I ounce unsweetened chocolate, broken in half
¹/₂ **cup confectioners' sugar**
³/₄ **cup granulated sugar**
¹/₄ **cup cocoa powder**

I teaspoon vanilla extract
¹/₄ **teaspoon almond extract**
I egg
Pinch of salt
¹/₂ **teaspoon baking powder**
I cup all-purpose flour

Preheat oven to 350°F.

In a large, heavy-bottomed saucepan over medium heat, melt the butter. Add the almonds and cook about 2 minutes, until the nuts are lightly toasted. Remove from heat, add the chocolate, and stir until it is completely melted. Stir in the sugars, cocoa, extracts, egg, and salt until smooth.

Add the baking powder in pinches to break up any lumps and stir thoroughly. Stir in the flour until well combined.

Pour and scrape the batter into a 9-inch square baking pan. Moisten your hands and shake off excess water. Gently press the batter into an even layer with your fingertips, remoistening your fingers if they start to stick to the batter.

Bake for 20 minutes, until the cookie is firm and the edges appear dry. Remove from the oven and cool on a rack for at least 15 minutes. Cut into 25 squares.

Chocolate Peanut Jumbles

These chewy cookies give you three great flavor pairs in one: chocolate and peanut butter, oatmeal and brown sugar, raisins and chocolate chips. Don't worry about the absence of flour; that's one of their secrets.

MAKES 4 DOZEN COOKIES

¹/₄ pound (I stick) unsalted butter

2 ounces unsweetened chocolate, broken in pieces

I cup peanut butter, chunky or smooth

2 cups firmly packed dark brown sugar

I teaspoon vanilla extract

3 eggs

4 cups oatmeal, quick or old-fashioned

I jar (8 ounces) unsalted, dry-roasted peanuts

6 ounces semisweet chocolate chips

I cup raisins

Preheat oven to 350°F. Coat a 10 × 15 × 1-inch jellyroll pan with spray shortening.

In a large, heavy-bottomed saucepan over medium heat, melt the butter. Continue to cook about 2 minutes, stirring often, until the butter browns lightly. Remove from heat and stir in the chocolate until melted. Stir in the peanut butter until melted. Stir in the brown sugar, vanilla, and eggs. Stir in the oatmeal, peanuts, chocolate chips, and raisins.

Pour and scrape the batter into the prepared pan. Moisten your hands and shake off excess water. Gently press the batter into an even layer with your fingertips, remoistening your fingers if they start to stick to the batter.

Bake for 25 minutes, until the cookie is just set. Remove from the oven and cool on a rack for at least 15 minutes. Cut into 48 squares.

Gooey Mocha Walnut Bars

Incredible! Imagine a walnut pie with chocolate chips, shadowed by coffee and a hint of dark rum. As these cookies bake, the chocolate melts into the sweet, coffee-scented goo, the base turns crisp, and the walnuts rise to the surface where they're lacquered in caramel.

MAKES 16 COOKIES

1/4 pound (1 stick) unsalted butter
1 cup graham cracker crumbs
1/2 cup dark corn syrup
1/2 cup dark brown sugar
Pinch of salt
1 teaspoon instant coffee powder

1 teaspoon vanilla extract
1 tablespoon dark rum
2 eggs
2 cups walnut halves and pieces
12 ounces semisweet chocolate chips

Preheat oven to 375°F.

In a large, heavy-bottomed saucepan over medium-high heat, melt the butter and cook until lightly browned, stirring occasionally. Pour about half the butter into a 9-inch square baking pan. Tilt the pan to allow the butter to coat the bottom of the pan. Add the graham cracker crumbs and gently press into an even layer over the butter. Bake for 5 minutes.

Meanwhile, add the corn syrup, brown sugar, salt, instant coffee, vanilla, rum, and eggs to the butter remaining in the saucepan, and stir until blended. Stir in the walnuts.

Remove the pan from the oven. Scatter the chocolate chips evenly over the graham cracker layer, pour the walnut mixture over all, and gently spread evenly.

Bake for 30 minutes. Remove from the oven and cool on a rack for at least 30 minutes. Cut around the sides and cut into 16 squares. Remove carefully with a small spatula.

Chocolate Cobbles

Don't be alarmed by the abundance of chunks in the batter for these cookies. As the cookies bake, the marshmallows disappear, leaving behind a network of lace and a remarkably light texture.

MAKES 16 COOKIES

4 tablespoons (1/2 stick) unsalted butter
5 ounces semisweet chocolate, broken in pieces
1 cup sugar
2 tablespoons cocoa powder
1/4 teaspoon salt
1 teaspoon vanilla extract

3 eggs
1 teaspoon baking powder
1/3 cup all-purpose flour
1 cup walnut pieces
1 cup unsalted, dry-roasted peanuts
1 cup semisweet chocolate chips
2 cups mini-marshmallows

Preheat oven to 350°F. Line a 9-inch square baking pan with foil and coat with spray shortening.

In a large, heavy-bottomed saucepan over medium heat, begin melting the butter. When it is half melted, add the chocolate. Remove from the heat when the chocolate is half melted and stir until the butter and chocolate are completely melted.

Add the sugar, cocoa, salt, and vanilla, and stir until smooth. Beat in the eggs. Add the baking powder in pinches to break up any lumps and stir thoroughly. Stir in the flour until smooth and satiny. Stir in the walnuts, peanuts, chocolate chips, and marshmallows.

Pour and scrape the batter into the prepared pan. Bake for 25 minutes, until the top is dry, bubbly, and cracked, but a tester inserted in the center comes out with a moist crumb clinging to it. Do not overbake.

Remove from the oven and cool on a rack for 30 minutes. Cover with a cutting board and invert pan. Remove the foil and cut into 16 squares with a serrated knife, using a sawing motion.

One Giant Espresso Chocolate Chip Cookie

This super-large cookie is just plain fun. The dough is baked in a pie pan and cut into wedges, like a pizza—a great birthday cake.

MAKES 16 SERVINGS

¼ pound (1 stick) unsalted butter
1 tablespoon instant coffee or espresso powder
¾ cup dark brown sugar
½ teaspoon vanilla extract

1 egg
½ teaspoon baking soda
1 cup flour
1½ cups large semisweet chocolate chips or mega-morsels

Preheat oven to 375°F. Coat a 9-inch pie plate with spray shortening.

In a large, heavy-bottomed saucepan over medium heat, begin melting the butter. When it is half melted, remove pan from the heat and continue stirring until butter is completely melted.

Stir in the coffee or espresso powder, brown sugar, vanilla, and egg. Add the baking soda in pinches to break up any lumps and stir thoroughly. Stir in the flour just until well combined, then stir in the chocolate chips.

Pour and scrape the batter into the prepared plate. Moisten your hands and shake off excess water. Gently press the batter into an even layer with your fingertips, remoistening your fingers if they start to stick to the batter. Smooth the top.

Bake for 23 minutes, until the cookie is just set. Remove from the oven and cool on a rack for 10 minutes. Cut into 16 wedges.

One-Pot Cookies

Chocolate Sugar Cookies

This reminds me of an old-fashioned ice-cream parlor cookie. The recipe makes about 4 dozen medium-sized square or diamond-shaped cookies, but you can cut the dough into any shape using cookie cutters or a small knife.

MAKES 4 DOZEN COOKIES

¹/₄ pound (I stick) unsalted butter
³/₄ cup dark brown sugar
¹/₄ teaspoon salt
¹/₄ cup coffee (liquid, not powder)
I teaspoon vanilla extract

3 tablespoons cocoa powder
I egg
I teaspoon baking powder
I¹/₂ cups whole wheat flour
2 tablespoons granulated sugar

Preheat oven to 375°F. Coat a 10 × 15 × 1-inch jellyroll pan with spray shortening.

In a large, heavy-bottomed saucepan over medium heat, melt the butter. Continue cooking about 2 minutes, stirring often, until the butter browns lightly. Remove from heat.

Stir in the brown sugar, salt, coffee, vanilla, cocoa, and egg until well mixed. Add the baking powder in pinches to break up any lumps and stir thoroughly. Stir in the flour and beat well.

Pour and scrape the batter into the prepared pan. Moisten your hands and shake off excess water. Gently press the batter into an even layer with your fingertips, remoistening your fingers if they start to stick to the batter. Sprinkle the granulated sugar evenly over the top.

Bake for 12 to 15 minutes, until the edges are crisp and the center is firm. Remove from the oven and cool on a rack for 10 minutes. Cut into 48 squares or 48 diamonds by cutting on the diagonal.

Chocolate Hazelnut Shards

Because these cookies are thin, crisp, and delicate, make sure the batter is spread evenly in the pan, or you'll get extra-thin spots that could burn. Once the baked sheet has cooled, break it into large, irregular-shaped pieces as you would praline or peanut brittle.

Makes 24 servings

¼ pound (1 stick) unsalted butter
1 ounce unsweetened chocolate, broken in
  pieces
½ cup sugar

¼ teaspoon almond extract
1 egg
⅓ cup flour
½ cup ground hazelnuts

Preheat oven to 375°F.

In a large, heavy-bottomed saucepan over medium heat, melt the butter. When the butter is half melted, add the chocolate. Remove from the heat when the chocolate is half melted and stir until the butter and chocolate are completely melted. Stir in the sugar, almond extract, and egg until smooth. Stir in the flour and beat well.

Pour and scrape the batter into a 10 × 15 × 1-inch jellyroll pan. Tilt the pan to allow the batter to form a thin, even layer across the bottom of the pan. Scatter the ground hazelnuts evenly over the top.

Bake for 10 minutes, until just set. Remove from the oven and cool on a rack for 20 minutes. Cut or break into 2 dozen irregular-shaped pieces.

Licentious Chocolate Macaroon Jewels

These sweet, chewy bars are little more than chocolate and nuts. Their structure comes from the egg and condensed milk. The amount of milk is approximate, for it will decrease depending on the moistness of the coconut. Because you will need only enough milk to coat the solid ingredients, start with three-quarters of the can, and add more if needed. Also, make sure you use sweetened coconut. Unsweetened shredded coconut measures lighter than sweetened coconut.

MAKES 25 COOKIES

3¹/₂ cups sweetened shredded coconut
1 cup ground walnuts
2 tablespoons cocoa powder (preferably
  Dutch-processed)
1 teaspoon ground cinnamon

2 teaspoons finely grated orange peel
³/₄ to 1 can (14 ounces) sweetened
  condensed milk
1 teaspoon vanilla extract
1 egg

Preheat oven to 350°F. Line an 8-inch square baking pan with foil.

In a mixing bowl, combine the coconut, walnuts, cocoa, cinnamon, and orange peel. Add the condensed milk and mix until all of the dry ingredients are coated. (Depending on how moist the coconut is, you might not need to use the entire can of condensed milk.) Stir in the vanilla and the egg.

Pour and scrape the batter into the prepared pan and spread into an even layer. Bake for 30 minutes, until the top is dry and the center feels firm. Cool on a rack for 20 minutes. Cover with a cutting board and invert pan. Remove the pan. Carefully peel off the foil. Cut into 25 squares with a serrated knife.

Fruit & Nut Cookies

Watch the squirrels, fat as cats, cramming in one more calorie as they prepare for winter. Seeds, grains, even a scrap of bark will do in a pinch, but the real prize is a nut or a forgotten bit of dried fruit. Packed with protein, sweetness, and fragrant oils, dried fruit and nuts are treasure chests of flavor and nutrition.

We nibble, too: melon in summer and pumpkin pie as the air turns brisk. But it's in the winter when eating becomes serious. Then even the most zealous dieter hunkers down to bar cookies inundated with chunks of cashews or ground filberts, raisins or berry preserves, toasted walnuts or dried papaya.

The appearance of new dried fruit and more varied processing for nuts has made baking with these ingredients easier as well as innovative. Toasted, ground nuts become the base for a cookie crust or a crumb topping. Dried berries, including blueberries, cranberries, strawberries, and raspberries, replace traditional raisins and currants with their intense flavors and colors. Dried peaches, pears, cherries, mangoes, and papayas move effortlessly into recipes that once relied solely on prunes, dates, and figs.

The advantage of dried fruit and nuts over their fresh counterparts is what's missing—moisture. In order to maintain the crunchy, chewy, or crispy texture essential to most cookies, liquid must be kept to a minimum. This requirement has traditionally forced fruit (most of which is loaded with juice) into a secondary role: simmered thick and pasted between sheets of dough, puddled in a hollow like a jellied solitaire, or brushed on the finished cookie as a glaze. Dried fruit, however, can be mixed directly into a dough. Because the fruit is dehydrated, its flavors are intensified, allowing a baker to either stud a cookie with vibrant morsels of fruit or grind the fruit right into the dough.

The same two options work for nuts, too, especially now that most nuts are available ground. If you can't find a particular nut ground, it is easy to grind nuts in a food processor or mini-chopper (see page 4). Just make sure you don't overload the work bowl, which results in uneven chopping.

The flavor of any nut is intensified by toasting, a process the one-pot method makes effortless. Add ground or chopped nuts to the melting butter, which is heated until the nuts toast uniformly. Be sure to stir the nuts constantly as they toast.

Several recipes in this chapter use a timesaving method developed for a crumbly pastry mixture in *One-Pot Cakes*. Some of that mixture is pressed into the baking pan and covered with preserves, pie filling, or pastry filling. The filling seeps into the pastry as it bakes, helping the pastry solidify. The remaining pastry is sprinkled over the filling, where it bakes into a streusel-style crumble.

Spiced Apricot Bars

These bars are remarkable. Built from layers of spiced pastry, sweetened apricot filling, and a nut streusel topping, they are effortlessly assembled in a single pot. They will stay fresh for a week at room temperature.

MAKES 16 COOKIES

¹/₄ pound (1 stick) unsalted butter
¹/₂ cup dark brown sugar
1 teaspoon ground cinnamon
Pinch of ground cloves
1 tablespoon dried lemon peel

Pinch of salt
1¹/₂ cups ground almonds
1 cup flour
¹/₂ cup apricot preserves

Preheat oven to 375°F. Coat a 9-inch square baking pan with spray shortening and dust with flour.

In a large, heavy-bottomed saucepan over medium heat, melt the butter, stirring occasionally. Remove from heat and stir in the sugar, cinnamon, cloves, lemon peel, salt, almonds, and flour until a dry, crumbly dough forms.

Press about half the dough into an even layer in the bottom of the prepared pan. Spread the preserves evenly over the dough, right up to the edges. Break the remaining dough into small pieces and scatter evenly over the top.

Bake 30 minutes, until light brown. Remove from the oven and cool on a rack for 20 minutes. Cut into 16 squares.

One-Pot Cookies

Linzer Bars

These delicate crumb-topped cookies take their name and flavor from Linzer torte, a famous tart of raspberry filling baked between layers of spiced nut pastry. Using whole wheat flour (besides providing nutrition) is essential for a toasted flavor.

MAKES 16 COOKIES

$^1/_4$ **pound (1 stick) unsalted butter**
$^1/_2$ **cup dark brown sugar**
1 teaspoon ground cinnamon
Pinch of ground cloves
1 tablespoon dried lemon peel

Pinch of salt
1 cup ground almonds
$^3/_4$ **cup cornstarch**
$^3/_4$ **cup whole wheat flour**
$^1/_4$ **cup seedless raspberry preserves**

Preheat oven to 375°F. Coat a 9-inch baking pan with spray shortening.

In a large, heavy-bottomed saucepan over medium heat, melt the butter, stirring occasionally. Remove from heat and stir in the sugar, cinnamon, cloves, lemon peel, salt, almonds, cornstarch, and flour until a dry, crumbly dough forms.

Press about half the dough into an even layer in the bottom of the prepared pan. Spread the preserves evenly over the dough right up to the edges. Break the remaining dough into small pieces and scatter evenly over the top.

Bake 30 minutes, until light brown. Remove from the oven and cool on a rack for 20 minutes. Cut into 16 squares and remove from the pan with a small spatula.

Ginger-Peachy Praline Bars

These crumb cookies are reminiscent of peach crisp. Pecans are toasted in the butter and then sweetened with sugar. Part of the pecan mixture is packed into the pan, where it forms the crust. The rest is scattered over the fruit, where it toasts into a delicate streusel topping.

MAKES 25 COOKIES

6 tablespoons (³/₄ stick) butter
¹/₂ cup ground pecans
6 tablespoons sugar
1 teaspoon ground ginger

Pinch of salt
1 cup flour
12 ounces peach preserves

Preheat oven to 375°F.

In a large, heavy-bottomed saucepan over medium heat, begin melting the butter. When it is half melted, add the pecans and stir often until the butter and nuts brown lightly. Remove from heat and stir in the sugar, ginger, salt, and flour until a dry, crumbly dough forms.

Press about two-thirds of the dough into an even layer in the bottom of an 8-inch square baking pan. Spread the preserves evenly over the dough, right up to the edges. Break the remaining dough into small pieces and scatter evenly over the top.

Bake 30 minutes, until you see bubbling around the edges and the dough is lightly browned on top. Remove from the oven and cool on a rack for 20 minutes. Run a knife around the edge and cut into 25 small squares.

Pecan Pie Bars

Gooey caramel filling, toasted nuts, and a cookie crumb crust make these mini–pecan pies a miraculous one-pot concoction. The graham cracker crust is made right in the baking pan and topped with a liquor-laced, pecan-permeated brown sugar ooze. Be careful not to overbake. When done, the filling should still be tacky in the center. Serve the edges to those who want more crunch, the center bars to those who don't mind slurping.

MAKES 16 COOKIES

1/4 pound (1 stick) unsalted butter
1 cup graham cracker crumbs
1 tablespoon dried orange peel
1/2 cup dark corn syrup
1/2 cup dark brown sugar

Pinch of salt
1 teaspoon vanilla extract
1 tablespoon brandy or bourbon
2 eggs
2 cups pecan halves

Preheat oven to 400°F.

In a large, heavy-bottomed saucepan over medium heat, melt the butter and cook until lightly browned, stirring occasionally. Pour about half of the butter into a 9-inch square baking pan. Tilt the pan to allow the butter to coat the bottom of the pan. Add the graham cracker crumbs and gently press into an even layer over the butter.

Add the orange peel, corn syrup, sugar, salt, vanilla, liquor, and eggs to the butter remaining in the saucepan. Stir until blended. Stir in the pecans. Pour the pecan mixture over the layer of graham cracker crumbs. Gently press into an even layer.

Bake for 30 minutes. Remove from the oven and cool on a rack for at least 30 minutes. Cut around the sides and cut into 16 squares. Remove carefully with a small spatula.

Apple Streusel Bars

These bars are bites of apple pie with a lemony streusel topping. If the can of apple pie filling you have is slightly larger or smaller than the one called for, use it anyway. A couple of ounces one way or the other will barely amount to one extra apple slice.

MAKES 16 COOKIES

6 tablespoons (³/₄ stick) unsalted butter
6 tablespoons light brown sugar
1 teaspoon cinnamon
Pinch of salt

1 cup plus 2 tablespoons flour
¹/₂ cup oatmeal, quick or old-fashioned
1 tablespoon dried lemon peel
1 can (1 pound, 5 ounces) apple pie filling

Preheat oven to 375°F.

In a large, heavy-bottomed saucepan over medium heat, melt the butter, stirring occasionally. Remove from the heat and stir in the sugar, cinnamon, salt, flour, oatmeal, and lemon peel until a dry, crumbly dough forms.

Press about two-thirds of the dough into an even layer in the bottom of a 9-inch square baking pan. Spread the pie filling evenly over the dough, right up to the edges. Break the remaining dough into small pieces and scatter evenly over the top.

Bake 30 minutes, until lightly browned. Remove from the oven and cool on a rack for 20 minutes. Cut into 16 squares.

Almond Sandbars

These delicate shortbread cookies get their brittle yet yielding consistency from confectioners' sugar. Confectioners' (or 10X) sugar is finely ground granulated sugar. The fineness makes the sugar extra sensitive to moisture and gives it a tendency to form lumps. To ensure this doesn't happen, the confectioners' sugar is mixed with cornstarch, which absorbs moisture, thus keeping it from the sugar. The cornstarch has an added benefit: By bonding with the flour in the recipe, it keeps the dough from becoming tough.

MAKES 25 COOKIES

¹/₄ **pound (1 stick) unsalted butter**	**1 egg**
¹/₂ **cup confectioners' sugar**	**Pinch of salt**
¹/₂ **cup granulated sugar**	**1 teaspoon baking powder**
¹/₈ **teaspoon almond extract**	**1¹/₂ cups flour**
¹/₂ **teaspoon vanilla extract**	**1 cup finely chopped almonds**

Preheat oven to 350°F. Coat a 9-inch square baking pan with spray shortening.

In a large, heavy-bottomed saucepan over medium heat, melt the butter. Remove from heat and stir in the sugars, extracts, egg, and salt until smooth.

Add the baking powder in pinches to break up any lumps and stir thoroughly. Stir in the flour and almonds until well combined.

Pour and scrape batter into the prepared pan. Moisten your hands and shake off excess water. Gently press the batter into an even layer with your fingertips, remoistening your fingers if they start to stick to the batter.

Bake for 25 minutes, until the edges are golden brown and the cookie is just set. Remove from the oven and cool on a rack for at least 15 minutes. Cut into 25 squares.

Dried Cherry Chunkies

Make sure you use dried sour (or red) cherries for these cookies. Their strong fruitiness and subtle tartness are essential to the full fruit flavor.

MAKES 3 DOZEN COOKIES

12 tablespoons (1½ sticks) unsalted butter

⅓ cup granulated sugar

1½ cups flour

¾ cup light brown sugar

3 eggs

1 tablespoon dried orange peel

1 teaspoon vanilla extract

1 cup chopped walnuts

1 cup dried sour (or red) cherries

Preheat oven to 350°F. Coat a 9-inch square baking pan with spray shortening.

In a large, heavy-bottomed saucepan over medium heat, melt the butter. Stir in the granulated sugar and flour until a smooth, thick dough forms.

Place all but 3 to 4 tablespoons of the dough into the prepared pan. Moisten your hands and shake off excess water. Gently press the dough into an even layer with your fingertips, remoistening your fingers if they start to stick to the dough. Bake for 10 minutes until the dough has a pale, golden color.

Meanwhile, add the brown sugar to the dough in the saucepan. Mix well. Mix in the eggs, orange peel, vanilla, walnuts, and dried cherries. Pour into the baking pan over the layer of baked pastry and smooth into an even layer.

Return pan to the oven and bake for 20 minutes. Remove from the oven and cool on a rack for at least 15 minutes. Cut into 36 squares and remove the cookies with a small spatula.

Marzipan Chews

The four ingredients that create these bite-size macaroons combine in minutes, which can be reduced to seconds if you use a food processor. Either way, your tiny culinary effort yields sophisticated results. Because these cookies have almost no fat, they tend to stick, so it is best to line your baking pan with foil. Remove the foil with the cookies, then peel the foil from the back of the baked sheet of cookies before cutting into squares.

MAKES 64 BITE-SIZED COOKIES OR 20 LARGE COOKIES

6 tablespoons confectioners' sugar
1 roll (7 ounces or about ³/₄ cup)
  marzipan

1 egg
¹/₂ cup finely ground almonds

Preheat oven to 325°F. Line an 8-inch square baking pan with foil, coat with spray shortening, and sprinkle with 2 tablespoons of the confectioners' sugar. This will be a thick coat, not a dusting.

In a mixing bowl, using a wooden spoon, combine the marzipan, egg, and almonds to make a thick dough.

Place the dough in the prepared pan. Moisten your hands and shake off excess water. Gently press the dough into an even layer with your fingertips, remoistening your fingers if they start to stick to the dough.

Bake for 18 minutes, until golden brown. Remove from the oven and cool on a rack for 5 minutes. Cover with a cutting board and invert pan. Remove the pan and peel the foil from the back of the cookie. Cut into 64 small squares or 20 triangles.

Note: This dough is easily mixed in a food processor. Just combine all the ingredients and process in 10 short pulses.

Macaroon Fingers

These macaroon bars are exceptionally moist and lightly chewy. Their one drawback is they stick mercilessly, so you must line the pan with foil. When the cookies are almost cool, invert the pan, remove the layer of cookies, and carefully peel the foil off the cookies. Don't worry if you have to rip the foil in order to get it off without damaging the cookies.

MAKES 24 COOKIES

14 ounces (3½ cups) sweetened shredded
  coconut
1 cup ground almonds
³/₄ to 1 can (14 ounces) sweetened
  condensed milk

½ teaspoon vanilla extract
¼ teaspoon almond extract
1 egg

Preheat oven to 350°F. Line an 8-inch square baking pan with foil.

In a mixing bowl, combine the coconut and the almonds. Add the sweetened condensed milk and mix until all the dry ingredients have been well coated. (Depending on the moistness of the coconut, you might not need to use the entire can of condensed milk.) Stir in the extracts and the egg until all ingredients are blended.

Pour and scrape the batter into the prepared pan. Moisten your hands and shake off excess water. Spread into an even layer, remoistening your fingers if they start to stick to the batter. Bake for 30 minutes, until the top is dry and the center feels firm. Remove from the oven and cool on a rack for 20 minutes. Cover with a cutting board and invert pan. Remove the pan. Carefully peel off the foil. Cut with a serrated knife into 24 rectangles.

Cranberry Tea Squares

Start these rich, mildly sweetened, white chocolate blondies by plumping the dried cranberries in boiling water. Then add the butter to the pot and continue as you would for any one-pot baking recipe. Dried cranberries, or Craisins, are available in supermarkets and health-food stores.

MAKES 16 COOKIES

1 cup dried cranberries
$^1/_2$ cup water
$^1/_4$ pound (1 stick) unsalted butter
2 ounces white chocolate
$^1/_2$ cup sugar

3 eggs
$^1/_4$ cup Triple Sec or other orange liqueur
$^2/_3$ cup ground hazelnuts
1 teaspoon vanilla extract
$^1/_2$ teaspoon baking powder

Preheat oven to 350°F. Line an 8-inch square baking pan with foil and coat with spray shortening.

In a large, heavy-bottomed saucepan over medium heat, combine the cranberries and water. Cook about 2 minutes, until all the water has been absorbed. Add the butter and begin melting it. When butter is half melted, add the chocolate. When the chocolate is half melted, remove the pan from the heat and stir until butter and chocolate are completely melted. Mix in the sugar, eggs, liqueur, hazelnuts, and vanilla. Add the baking powder in pinches to break up any lumps and stir thoroughly.

Pour and scrape the batter into the prepared pan. Bake for 25 minutes, until springy in the center. Remove from the oven and cool on a rack for 20 minutes. Cover with a cutting board and invert pan. Remove the pan. Peel the foil from the cookie. Cool to room temperature and cut with a serrated knife into 16 squares, using a sawing motion.

Oatmeal & Other Whole-Grain Cookies

Health and cookies don't mix. Strip a cookie of fat and sugar, pump it up with wheat germ, or douse it with beta-carotene, and it loses its identity. It becomes just another food: something nutritionists count, something you have to finish before you get dessert.

But that doesn't mean a luscious cookie can't benefit from a little whole grain—not for nutrition but for flavor. Whole wheat, for example, is nutty, toasted, and bittersweet, with an aroma and flavor that make brown sugar tilt toward caramel. Oatmeal is creamy and soft, and adds chewiness and dairy richness without adding fat. The grit of cornmeal makes a popcorn-scented shortbread that's the perfect amalgam of crumble and crunch. Bulgur, pre-cooked whole grains of wheat that are cracked and dried, acts like oatmeal in a cookie. Buckwheat underscores the earthiness of a molasses cookie, and oat flour preserves softness and slows staling.

The drawback of whole grains is that they tend to rise poorly, inflicting an unappealing density on leavened baked goods such as cakes and breads. But because most cookies rise only minimally, we can enjoy the flavor and texture of a grain without its leaden downside.

Oatmeal is the most common of whole grains used for cookies. Use only quick or old-fashioned rolled oats. Instant oatmeal is too finely ground to work properly, and cut oatmeal (or Irish oatmeal) is too coarse.

In addition to oat cookies, we have recipes for a shortbread made from corn, a homemade version of graham crackers that are slightly thicker and a bit plusher than commercially made varieties, a wheat germ brownie that tastes like butterscotch, and an exotic mint and lemon cookie you'd never guess was made from a box of tabbouleh salad mix.

Molasses Oat Chewies

These large, dark, soft, chewy cookies radiate molasses. They have an old-fashioned flavor and feel, and the molasses helps keep them moist in a cookie jar for well over a week.

MAKES 2 DOZEN COOKIES

1/4 **pound (1 stick) unsalted butter**	2 **eggs**
3/4 **cup dark brown sugar**	2 **teaspoons baking powder**
3/4 **cup granulated sugar**	1 3/4 **cups flour**
1/4 **cup light or dark molasses**	2 **cups oatmeal, quick or old-fashioned**
Pinch of salt	**(not instant or cut)**
1 **teaspoon vanilla extract**	1 **cup raisins**
1/2 **teaspoon ground cinnamon**	

Preheat oven to 350°F. Coat a 10 × 15 × 1-inch jellyroll pan with spray shortening.

In a large, heavy-bottomed saucepan over medium heat, melt the butter. Remove from heat and stir in the sugars, molasses, salt, vanilla, cinnamon, and eggs.

Add the baking powder in pinches to break up any lumps and stir thoroughly. Stir in the flour until a smooth batter forms. Fold in the oatmeal and raisins until they are evenly distributed.

Pour and scrape the batter into the prepared pan. Moisten your hands and shake off excess water. Gently press the batter into an even layer with your fingertips, remoistening your fingers if they start to stick to the batter.

Bake for 18 to 20 minutes, until the edges are browned and the cookie is just set. Remove from the oven and cool on a rack for at least 15 minutes. Slice into 24 squares.

Chocolate Chocolate Chip Oatmeal Bars

These thick chocolate oatmeal bricks are a cross between an oatmeal cookie and a brownie.

Makes 25 cookies

1/4 **pound (1 stick) unsalted butter**	**Pinch of salt**
1 cup dark brown sugar	**1 egg**
1/4 **cup cocoa powder**	1/2 **teaspoon baking soda**
1 cup oatmeal, quick or old-fashioned	1/4 **cup flour**
(not instant or cut)	**6 ounces semisweet chocolate chips**
1 teaspoon vanilla extract	

Preheat oven to 350°F. Coat a 9-inch square baking pan with spray shortening.

In a large, heavy-bottomed saucepan over medium heat, melt the butter. Stir in the brown sugar, cocoa, oatmeal, vanilla, salt, and egg. Add the baking soda in pinches to break up any lumps and stir thoroughly. Stir in the flour until a stiff dough forms. Mix in the chocolate chips.

Pour and scrape the dough into the prepared pan. Moisten your hands and shake off excess water. Gently press the dough into an even layer with your fingertips, remoistening your fingers if they start to stick to the dough. Smooth the top.

Bake for 20 minutes, until a tester inserted into the center comes out with just a few moist crumbs clinging to it. Slice into 25 squares and remove them with a small spatula.

Orange-Cranberry Oat Bars

Soften the dried cranberries for these cookies in liqueur. If you'd rather not use liqueur, substitute orange juice or water. These blondies are moist and will stay that way for days in a cookie jar.

Makes 25 cookies

1 cup dried cranberries (or Craisins)	1 cup sugar
¼ cup Triple Sec or other orange-flavored liqueur	½ teaspoon vanilla extract
	¼ teaspoon orange extract
¼ pound (1 stick) unsalted butter	Pinch of salt
1½ cups oatmeal, quick or old-fashioned (not instant or cut)	1 egg
	1 teaspoon baking powder
2 teaspoons dried orange peel	1 cup flour

Preheat oven to 350°F. Coat a 9-inch square baking pan with spray shortening.

In a large, heavy-bottomed saucepan over medium heat, cook the dried cranberries in the liqueur until most of the liqueur has been absorbed. Add the butter and heat until melted. Remove from heat and stir in the oatmeal, orange peel, sugar, extracts, salt, and egg until smooth.

Add the baking powder in pinches to break up any lumps and stir thoroughly. Stir in the flour until well combined.

Pour and scrape the batter into the prepared pan and spread into an even layer. Bake for 20 minutes, until lightly browned and just set. Remove from the oven and cool on a rack for 30 minutes. Cut into 25 squares.

Butterscotch Oatmeal Whole Wheat Chews

The toasted flavor of whole wheat flour and butterscotch go together naturally. These gooey bars are loaded with butterscotch chips, but no one will guess you sneaked in whole wheat flour.

MAKES 16 LARGE COOKIES

$1/4$ **pound (1 stick) unsalted butter**
$1/2$ **cup oatmeal, quick or old-fashioned**
  (not instant or cut)
1 cup light brown sugar
1 teaspoon vanilla extract

1 egg
Pinch of salt
1 teaspoon baking powder
1 cup whole wheat flour
1 cup butterscotch morsels

Preheat oven to 350°F. Coat a 9-inch square baking pan with spray shortening.

In a large, heavy-bottomed saucepan over medium heat, melt the butter. Remove from heat and add the oatmeal, sugar, vanilla, egg, and salt. Stir until smooth.

Add the baking powder in pinches to break up any lumps and stir thoroughly. Stir in the flour until well combined. Stir in the butterscotch morsels.

Pour and scrape the batter into the prepared pan. Moisten your hands and shake off excess water. Gently press the batter into an even layer with your fingertips, remoistening your fingers if they start to stick to the batter.

Bake for 17 minutes, until browned and just set. Remove from the oven and cool on a rack for 30 minutes. Cut into 16 squares.

Peanut Butter Oatmeal Peanut Bars

These big, thick, fabulous cookies contain no flour, just a ton of oatmeal, raisins, and peanuts held together by faith and a little brown sugar goo. They do not go stale—they never last that long.

<small>Makes 2 dozen cookies</small>

¼ pound (1 stick) unsalted butter	**1 teaspoon vanilla extract**
1½ cups peanut butter, crunchy or	**3 eggs**
smooth	**4½ cups quick or old-fashioned oatmeal**
1 cup dark brown sugar	**(not instant or cut)**
1 cup granulated sugar	**2 cups raisins**
Pinch of salt	**2 cups unsalted, roasted peanuts**

Preheat oven to 350°F. Coat a 10 × 15 × 1-inch jellyroll pan with spray shortening and dust with flour.

In a large, heavy-bottomed saucepan over medium heat, begin melting the butter. When it's about half melted, add the peanut butter and continue stirring until the butter and peanut butter are completely melted.

Remove from heat and stir in the sugars, salt, vanilla, and eggs. Stir in the oatmeal, then the raisins and peanuts.

Pour and scrape the batter into the prepared pan. Moisten your hands and shake off excess water. Gently press the batter into an even layer with your fingertips, remoistening your fingers if they start to stick to the batter.

Bake for 23 minutes, until just set. Remove from the oven and cool on a rack for at least 15 minutes. Cut into 12 large squares and cut each square in half diagonally.

Dark Chocolate Oat Wafers

Extremely thin, extremely chocolaty, extremely delicate, these cookies are sprinkled with rolled oats. Thin spots can burn, so make sure the batter is spread evenly over the pan. Store the cookies in a tightly covered container to preserve their crispness.

MAKES 2 DOZEN COOKIES

$^1/_4$ pound (1 stick) unsalted butter
1 ounce unsweetened chocolate, broken in half
$^1/_2$ cup sugar
$^1/_2$ teaspoon ground cinnamon

$^1/_4$ teaspoon vanilla extract
1 egg
$^1/_3$ cup flour
1 cup oatmeal, quick or old-fashioned (not instant or cut)

Preheat oven to 375°F.

In a large, heavy-bottomed saucepan over medium heat, begin melting the butter. When it is half melted, add the chocolate. Remove from heat when the chocolate is half melted and stir until the butter and chocolate are completely melted.

Stir in the sugar, cinnamon, vanilla, and egg. The mixture may look as if it has separated slightly; this is OK. Stir in the flour and oatmeal and beat well until smooth.

Pour and scrape the batter into a 10 × 15 × 1-inch jellyroll pan. Spread batter into a thin, even layer. Bake for 10 minutes, until just set. Remove from the oven and cool on a rack for 20 minutes. Cut into 24 squares.

Pecan Corn Sablés

"Sablé" means "sandy" in French, an allusion to the crumbly nature of these shortbread cookies. The fattiness shortbreads are prone to is cut here by the delicate grit of the cornmeal.

MAKES 25 COOKIES

₁/₄ pound (I stick) unsalted butter
I cup pecan pieces
I teaspoon dried orange or lemon peel
³/₄ cup confectioners' sugar
I teaspoon vanilla extract

Pinch of salt
I egg
I cup cornmeal
¹/₂ cup whole wheat flour

Preheat oven to 350°F. Coat a 9-inch square baking pan with spray shortening.

In a large, heavy-bottomed saucepan over medium heat, melt the butter. Add the pecan pieces and cook about 2 minutes, until the nuts toast lightly. Remove from heat and stir in the citrus peel, sugar, vanilla, salt, and egg. Mix until smooth. Stir in the cornmeal and flour until a smooth batter forms.

Pour and scrape the batter into the prepared pan. Moisten your hands and shake off excess water. Gently press the batter into an even layer with your fingertips, remoistening your fingers if they start to stick to the batter. Bake for 18 to 20 minutes, until lightly browned and just set. Remove from the oven and cool on a rack for 30 minutes. Cut into 25 squares.

Wheat Germ Brownies

In these brownies, whole wheat flour is enriched with wheat germ. The miracle is that they come out tasting exactly like butterscotch brownies. (I won't tell if you won't.)

MAKES 16 BROWNIES

¹/₄ **pound (1 stick) unsalted butter**	**Pinch of salt**
1 cup wheat germ	**1 egg**
1 cup light brown sugar	**1 teaspoon baking powder**
1 teaspoon vanilla extract	**1 cup whole wheat flour**

Preheat oven to 350°F. Coat a 9-inch square baking pan with spray shortening.

In a large, heavy-bottomed saucepan over medium heat, melt the butter. Remove from heat and stir in the wheat germ, sugar, vanilla, salt, and egg until smooth. Add the baking powder in pinches to break up any lumps and stir thoroughly. Stir in the flour until a smooth batter forms.

Pour and scrape the batter into the prepared pan and spread into an even layer. Bake for 17 minutes, until browned and just set. Remove from the oven and cool on a rack for 30 minutes. Cut into 16 squares.

Graham Cookies

These ultra-plain, lightly sweetened graham cookies taste like homemade graham crackers and are perfect served with a glass of cold milk. Softer and thicker than commercial graham crackers, these are lightly scented with vanilla and, because of the brown sugar, some molasses.

MAKES 4 DOZEN COOKIES

¹/₄ **pound (I stick) unsalted butter**	**I teaspoon vanilla extract**
³/₄ **cup dark brown sugar**	**I egg**
¹/₄ **teaspoon salt**	**I teaspoon baking powder**
¹/₄ **cup milk**	**I¹/₂ cups whole wheat flour**

Preheat oven to 375°F. Coat a 10 × 15 × 1-inch jellyroll pan with spray shortening.

In a large, heavy-bottomed saucepan over medium heat, melt the butter. Stir in the brown sugar, salt, milk, vanilla, and egg until well combined. Add the baking powder in pinches to break up any lumps and stir thoroughly. Stir in the flour and beat well.

Pour and scrape the batter into the prepared pan. Moisten your hands and shake off excess water. Gently press the batter into an even layer with your fingertips, remoistening your fingers if they start to stick to the batter.

Bake for 12 to 15 minutes, until the edges are browned and the center is firm. Remove from the oven and cool on a rack for 10 minutes. Cut into 48 squares or diamonds by cutting on the diagonal.

Tabbouleh Chews

This cookie will surprise you as much as it surprised me. I started working with bulgur wheat alone and got adequate results: a pleasant oatmeal-cookie texture with the flavor of whole wheat. I retested the recipe using a box of tabbouleh with the herbs and spices for a salad blended with bulgur. I was amazed to find that the mint and lemon came alive when sweetened and combined with a little cinnamon and some dried currants. Who knew?

MAKES 2 DOZEN COOKIES

1/4 pound (1 stick) unsalted butter	1 1/2 cups sugar
1 cup walnut pieces	1 teaspoon ground cinnamon
2 tablespoons dried lemon peel	Pinch of salt
1 cup dried currants	1 tablespoon lemon juice
1 cup (a 2 1/2-ounce box) tabbouleh (see	2 eggs
Note on next page)	1/4 teaspoon baking powder
1 cup water	1 1/2 cups whole wheat flour

Preheat oven to 350°F. Coat a 10 × 15 × 1-inch jellyroll pan with spray shortening.

In a large, heavy-bottomed saucepan over medium heat, melt the butter. Add the walnuts and stir about 2 minutes, until nuts are lightly toasted. Remove from heat and stir in the lemon peel, currants, tabbouleh, and water. Let sit for 3 minutes, then stir in the sugar, cinnamon, salt, lemon juice, and eggs.

Add the baking powder in pinches to break up any lumps and stir thoroughly. Stir in the flour until a smooth batter forms.

Pour and scrape the batter into the prepared pan. Moisten your hands and shake off excess water. Gently press the batter into an even layer with your fingertips, remoistening your fingers if they start to stick to the batter. Bake for 22 to 25 minutes, until the edges are browned and the cookie is just set. Remove from the oven and cool on a rack for at least 15 minutes. Cut into 24 squares.

Note: Tabbouleh is a Middle Eastern grain salad made from bulgur wheat. Bulgur is cracked whole wheat that is steamed and then dried. You will find tabbouleh and bulgur with other grains, such as rice and barley, in your market. This recipe is made from a tabbouleh mix that is fully seasoned. Depending on the brand you buy, the flavorings will be mixed in with the bulgur or in a separate spice pack. If the flavorings are packed separately, just add them with the tabbouleh.

Shortbreads

Shortbread is a cookie honed to its essentials: butter, sugar, and flour. No eggs or leaven to let it stretch and rise, no milk or cream to make it more like cake. Occasionally it may, in the interest of panache, endure a smattering of nuts or the scent of citrus, but a shortbread's inventory usually is brief.

Don't let the lean ingredients list fool you. Shortbreads are by far the plushest, richest, and fattest of cookie formulas and some of the most decadent and sophisticated of all cookies.

By converting shortbreads to a one-pot method, we make the most of the few elements' versatility. Melting the butter for a shortbread, rather than beating it into the dough, for example, lets you reduce the amount of fat by up to 20 percent. The melted butter can be browned, giving the shortbread a rich caramel color and flavor. Using light or dark brown sugar further intensifies the roasted, caramelized flavors. Adding ground nuts to the browning butter makes shortbreads redolent of toasted almond or sesame.

Shortbreads often use cake flour or a combination of all-purpose flour and cornstarch to ensure the dough stays soft and the cookie tender. Feel free to use either option ($2^1/_3$ cups cake flour is equivalent to 2 cups all-purpose flour blended with $^1/_3$ cup cornstarch).

Shortbreads will be quite soft when they emerge from the oven and get crisper as they cool. It is best to cut the dough into cookies before they reach room temperature to keep them from crumbling. Do this either by making perforated lines in the cookie dough with the tines of a fork before it is baked or by slicing the shortbread while the baked sheet is still warm. (Usually, thinner shortbreads are perforated; thicker ones are cut after baking.)

Some shortbreads call for baking powder to lighten recipes that might be too dense. In this chapter, I have added small amounts of leaven when a shortbread is loaded with nuts (Ginger Sesame Shortcakes, page 63), flavored with chocolate (Chocolate Cinnamon Shortbread, page 62), or has an unusual texture (Cashew Shortbread Biscotti, page 65).

Lemon Walnut Shortbread

This refreshing shortbread is brimming with the flavor of toasted walnuts. The method prevents the nuts from becoming too dark and overshadowing the lemon.

MAKES 2 DOZEN COOKIES

½ pound (2 sticks) unsalted butter
2 cups ground walnuts
1 tablespoon dried lemon peel

⅔ cup sugar
1 teaspoon vanilla extract
2⅓ cups cake flour

Preheat oven to 375°F.

In a large, heavy-bottomed saucepan over medium heat, begin melting the butter. When it is half melted, add the walnuts and lemon peel and continue stirring until the butter is completely melted. Remove from heat and stir in the sugar and vanilla. Add the flour and stir about 30 seconds, until a smooth, stiff dough forms.

Place the dough in a 10 × 15 × 1-inch jellyroll pan. Moisten your hands and shake off all excess water. Gently press the dough into an even layer with your fingertips, remoistening your fingers if they start to stick to the dough. With a fork, mark off 24 diamond-shaped bars, piercing diagonal perforated lines through the dough.

Bake for 20 minutes, until lightly browned. Remove from the oven and cool to room temperature. Cut along the perforated lines to separate into serving pieces.

Brown Butter Shortbread

The incredible caramel flavor of this shortbread is all in the technique. Don't let the heat get too high or the butter will brown unevenly.

MAKES 2 DOZEN COOKIES

¹/₂ pound (2 sticks) unsalted butter
²/₃ cup ground pecans or almonds
1 cup dark brown sugar

¹/₄ teaspoon vanilla extract
2 cups flour
¹/₃ cup cornstarch

Preheat oven to 375°F.

In a large, heavy-bottomed saucepan over medium heat, begin melting the butter. When it is half melted, add the nuts and continue stirring often until the butter is completely melted and has turned a deep brown. Remove from heat and stir in the sugar and vanilla. Add the flour and cornstarch and stir about 30 seconds, until a smooth, stiff dough forms.

Place the dough in a 10 × 15 × 1-inch jellyroll pan. Moisten your hands and shake off excess water. Gently press the dough into an even layer with your fingertips, remoistening your fingers if they start to stick to the dough. With a fork, mark off 24 diamond-shaped bars, piercing diagonal perforated lines through the dough.

Bake for 15 minutes, until brown at the edges. Remove from the oven and cool on a rack to room temperature. Cut along the perforated lines to separate into serving pieces.

Pistachio-Cardamom Butter Cookies

Fragrant and rich, these exotically flavored cookies cry out for a big cup of strong, sweet tea. Cardamom tastes a little like ginger without the spiciness.

MAKES 2 DOZEN COOKIES

¹/₂ **pound (2 sticks) unsalted butter**
1 generous cup shelled pistachios,
   chopped into medium pieces
³/₄ **cup sugar**

2 teaspoons ground cardamom
¹/₂ **teaspoon ground ginger**
¹/₄ **teaspoon vanilla extract**
2¹/₃ **cups cake flour**

Preheat oven to 375°F.

In a large, heavy-bottomed saucepan over medium heat, begin melting the butter. When it is half melted, add the pistachios and continue stirring until the butter is completely melted. Remove from heat and stir in the sugar, cardamom, ginger, and vanilla. Stir in the flour, about 30 seconds, until a smooth, stiff dough forms.

Place the dough in a 10 × 15 × 1-inch jellyroll pan. Moisten your hands and shake off excess water. Gently press the dough into an even layer with your fingertips, remoistening your fingers if they start to stick to the dough. With a fork, mark off 24 diamond-shaped bars, piercing diagonal perforated lines through the dough.

Bake for 20 minutes, until lightly browned. Remove from the oven and cool to room temperature. Cut along the perforated lines to separate into serving pieces.

Praline Sandies

These crumbly cookies have the flavor of praline and the consistency of butter. The buttermilk helps keep them soft. If you don't have buttermilk, substitute 2¹/₂ tablespoons of milk mixed with ¹/₄ teaspoon of vinegar or lemon juice.

MAKES 1 DOZEN LARGE AND 1 DOZEN SMALL COOKIES

¹/₄ pound (1 stick) unsalted butter
1¹/₄ cups ground pecans
¹/₂ cup light brown sugar
2 tablespoons buttermilk
1 teaspoon vanilla extract

1 cup flour
24 pecan pieces (12 halves and 12 broken pieces)
1 tablespoon granulated sugar

Preheat oven to 375°F.

In a large, heavy-bottomed saucepan over medium heat, melt the butter. Add the ground pecans and, stirring often, cook until the butter and nuts are lightly toasted. Remove from heat and stir in the brown sugar, buttermilk, and vanilla. Add the flour, stirring about 30 seconds, until a smooth, stiff dough forms.

Place the dough in a 9-inch square baking pan. Moisten your hands and shake off excess water. Gently press the dough into an even layer with your fingertips, remoistening your fingers if they start to stick to the dough. With a fork, mark off 12 diamond-shaped bars, piercing diagonal perforated lines through the dough. You will have 12 triangular pieces at the edges. Place a pecan half on each diamond and a broken pecan on each triangle. Sprinkle the surface with the granulated sugar.

Bake for 15 minutes, until lightly browned. Remove from the oven and cool on a rack for 10 minutes. Cut along the perforated lines to separate into serving pieces.

Orange Rosemary Shortbread

No one will guess where the floral fragrance and colorful speckles in these cookies come from. They're from rosemary, an ingredient you've probably never used in a cookie. And yet, the herb yields a spicy, mint flavor that's natural and subtle. Crush the dried rosemary with your fingers to release its flavor.

MAKES 2 DOZEN COOKIES

¹/₂ **pound (2 sticks) unsalted butter**	**1 cup sugar**
2 teaspoons crushed rosemary	**2 teaspoons lemon juice**
1 tablespoon dried orange peel	**2¹/₂ cups cake flour**

Preheat oven to 375°F.

In a large, heavy-bottomed saucepan over medium heat, melt the butter. Remove from heat, add the rosemary and orange peel, and stir to combine. Stir in the sugar and lemon juice. Stir in the flour, until a smooth, stiff dough forms.

Place the dough in a 10 × 15 × 1-inch jellyroll pan. Moisten your hands and shake off excess water. Gently press the dough into an even layer with your fingertips, remoistening your fingers if they start to stick to the dough. With a fork, mark off 24 diamond-shaped bars, piercing diagonal perforated lines through the dough.

Bake for 15 minutes. Remove from the oven and cool on a rack to room temperature. Cut along the perforated lines to separate into serving pieces.

Chocolate Cinnamon Shortbread

These dark chocolate, cinnamon-scented shortbread squares get their creamy consistency from the starch in the confectioners' sugar.

MAKES 25 COOKIES

¹/₄ pound (1 stick) unsalted butter
1 ounce unsweetened chocolate, broken in half
¹/₂ cup confectioners' sugar
³/₄ cup granulated sugar
1 teaspoon ground cinnamon

¹/₄ cup cocoa powder
1 teaspoon vanilla extract
1 egg
Pinch of salt
¹/₂ teaspoon baking powder
1 cup all-purpose flour

Preheat oven to 350°F.

In a large, heavy-bottomed saucepan over medium heat, begin melting the butter. When it is half melted, add the chocolate and continue cooking until the chocolate is half melted. Remove from heat and stir until butter and chocolate are completely melted.

Stir in the sugars, cinnamon, cocoa, vanilla, egg, and salt until smooth. Add the baking powder in pinches to break up any lumps and stir thoroughly. Stir in the flour until well combined.

Pour and scrape batter into a 9-inch square baking pan. Moisten your hands and shake off excess water. Gently press the batter into an even layer with your fingertips, remoistening your fingers if they start to stick to the batter.

Bake for 20 minutes, until firm and the edges appear dry. Remove from the oven and cool on a rack for at least 15 minutes. Cut into 25 squares.

Ginger Sesame Shortcakes

In this recipe, cakelike cubes of buttery shortbread are encased in toasted sesame seeds. The contrasting textures of seed and cake are wonderful.

MAKES 25 COOKIES

¹/₄ pound (I stick) unsalted butter
I¹/₂ cups toasted sesame seeds
I teaspoon ground ginger
³/₄ cup sugar
I tablespoon dark (toasted) sesame oil

I teaspoon vanilla extract
I egg
2 teaspoons baking powder
2 cups flour

Preheat oven to 350°F.

In a large, heavy-bottomed saucepan over medium heat, melt the butter. Remove from heat. Add I cup sesame seeds, the ginger, sugar, and sesame oil, and stir to combine. Stir in the vanilla and egg. Add the baking powder in pinches to break up any lumps and stir thoroughly. Stir in the flour until a smooth, stiff dough forms.

Pour and scrape the dough into an 8-inch square baking pan. Moisten your hands and shake off excess water. Gently press the dough into an even layer with your fingertips, remoistening your fingers if they start to stick to the dough. Sprinkle the remaining ¹/₂ cup sesame seeds over the surface of the dough and spread into an even layer with your fingertips.

Bake for 20 minutes. Remove from the oven and cool on a rack to room temperature. Cut into 25 squares.

Almond Cream-Cheese Shortbread

Cream cheese takes the place of some of the butter in these creamy cookies. They are reminiscent of old-fashioned cream cheese icebox cookies, but without the added refrigeration step.

MAKES 25 COOKIES

1/4 pound (1 stick) unsalted butter
1/2 cup ground almonds
8 ounces cream cheese
1 1/4 cups confectioners' sugar

1 teaspoon vanilla extract
1/4 teaspoon almond extract
2 cups flour

Preheat oven to 375°F.

In a large, heavy-bottomed saucepan over medium heat, begin melting the butter. Turn heat to low, add the ground almonds and the cream cheese, and stir until the butter is completely melted. Remove from heat and stir until the cream cheese is completely melted.

Stir in 1 cup confectioners' sugar, the extracts, and flour, mixing until a smooth, stiff dough forms.

Pour and scrape the dough into a 9-inch square baking pan. Moisten your hands and shake off excess water. Gently press the dough into an even layer with your fingertips, remoistening your fingers if they start to stick to the dough. With a fork, mark off 25 squares, piercing diagonal lines through the dough. Sprinkle with the remaining 1/4 cup of confectioners' sugar.

Bake for 20 minutes. Remove from the oven and cool on a rack to room temperature. Cut along the perforated lines into 25 squares.

Cashew Shortbread Biscotti

Think of these as either very tender biscotti or very crunchy shortbreads. But do give them a try, especially if you are a fan of cashews.

MAKES 16 COOKIES

¹/₄ pound (1 stick) unsalted butter
1¹/₂ cups unsalted cashew pieces or halves
¹/₂ cup sugar
1 teaspoon vanilla extract

1 egg
¹/₄ teaspoon baking powder
1¹/₄ cups flour

Preheat oven to 350°F. Coat a 9-inch square baking pan with spray shortening.

In a large, heavy-bottomed saucepan over medium heat, melt the butter. Add the cashews and cook until nuts are lightly toasted. Remove from heat and mix in sugar and vanilla. Beat in the egg. Add the baking powder in pinches to break up any lumps and stir thoroughly. Stir in the flour, until a smooth, stiff dough forms.

Pour and scrape the dough into the prepared pan. Moisten your hands and shake off excess water. Gently press the dough into an even layer with your fingertips, remoistening your fingers if they start to stick to the dough.

Bake for 20 minutes. Remove from the oven. Cover with a cutting board and invert pan. Remove the pan. Cut in half with a serrated knife and cut each half into 8 rectangular strips. Place the strips back in the pan, setting each strip on a narrow side. Return the pan to the oven and bake for 25 more minutes, until golden brown and crisp.

Chocolate Peanut Brittle

This is a crisp chocolate cookie topped with roasted peanuts. It's one of the only times I use salted nuts in baking, but they lend just the right counterpoint to the sweet chocolate cookie.

MAKES 2 DOZEN COOKIES

¼ pound (1 stick) unsalted butter
1 cup confectioners' sugar
½ cup cocoa powder

1¼ cups flour
¾ cup salted peanuts, dry-roasted

Preheat oven to 325°F.

In a large, heavy-bottomed saucepan over medium heat, melt the butter. Remove from heat. Add the sugar, cocoa, and flour, and stir until a smooth, stiff dough forms.

Pour and scrape the dough into a 10 × 15 × 1-inch jellyroll pan. Moisten your hands and shake off excess water. Gently press the dough into an even layer with your fingertips, re-moistening your fingers if they start to stick to the dough. Scatter the peanuts over the surface in an even layer and press them lightly into the surface of the dough.

Bake for 15 minutes, until the nuts are lightly toasted and the dough appears brittle at its edges. Remove from the oven and cool on a rack to room temperature. The cookies are fragile and have a tendency to break, so use a small, sharp knife to cut carefully through the peanuts. Cut on the diagonal into 24 diamonds.

Brownies, Blondies, & Beigies

Cookie-naming is a game. In the fewest possible words, you must fix within the imagination all the sensory charms your cookie has to offer. You can allude to texture (crispy, crunchy, cakey, gooey), appearance (lacy, chunky, pudgy), and flavor (chocolate, spiced, praline), but it's best when you can capture all these qualities in just one item.

Praise the brownie!

In a single word, the fudgy interior, the crackled skin, and the amalgam of chocolate and walnuts immediately come into imaginary view. No other cookie name conveys so much. Its power is equally accessible to its paler brethren. No one has to tell you that blondies or beigies are equally lush. It's enough that they are brownie clones.

The unique consistency of these bar cookies is a question of batter and baking. Chocolate has little to do with it. The batter is low in moisture and flour, which prevents brownies, blondies, and beigies from becoming cakey. Egg, which generally is the only liquid in the batter, makes them chewy; and fat, usually butter, keeps them soft. The relationship between the butter and the egg is what creates the soft, chewy interplay that makes brownies, blondies, and beigies so great.

Because the batter has so little liquid, the moisture content of the finished product is maintained by underbaking. A perfectly baked batch of brownies will have a thin crust, a crackled and slightly risen edge, and a center that is still damp. A toothpick or skewer used as a tester should emerge from the core with a bit of partially congealed batter clinging to it. This stickiness is the best sign that your steaming-hot brownies will remain decadently moist once they have cooled. A tester that comes out clean indicates a brownie that may taste great right out of the oven but one that will become hopelessly dry once it has cooled.

I use several different pans in these recipes. Most call for an 8- or 9-inch square baking pan. The size of the pan was chosen by the amount of batter in each recipe. Switching the pans will not be disastrous, but it will cause some difference in the final texture.

One-Pot Cookies

Dark Chocolate Brownies with Almonds

Ever since my first Hershey bar with almonds, I have been convinced that chocolate-cloaked nuts should be classified as an addictive substance. These brownies have the same irresistible allure. They can be stored on a covered plate at room temperature for 2 to 3 days. If you wrap the brownies individually, they can be stored at room temperature for up to a week. At my house, however, they never last that long. As all brownies do, these freeze well.

MAKES 4 DOZEN BROWNIES

2 cups unsalted whole almonds, with skins

$^1/_2$ pound (2 sticks) unsalted butter

6 ounces unsweetened chocolate, broken in pieces

1 teaspoon vanilla extract

$^1/_4$ teaspoon almond extract

$1^2/_3$ cups granulated sugar

$^2/_3$ cup dark brown sugar

$^1/_2$ cup dark corn syrup

5 eggs

2 cups flour

Preheat oven to 350°F. Place the almonds in a 10 × 15 × 1-inch jellyroll pan. Place pan in the oven about 7 minutes, while you prepare the batter.

In a large, heavy-bottomed saucepan over medium heat, begin melting the butter. When it is half melted, add the chocolate. Remove from heat when the chocolate is half melted and stir until the butter and chocolate are completely melted.

Stir in the extracts, sugars, corn syrup, and eggs. Stir in the flour, just until blended. Remove the almonds from the oven and mix into the batter.

Line the pan you used for the almonds with foil and coat with spray shortening. Pour and scrape the batter into the prepared pan and smooth the top. The batter will nearly fill the pan.

Bake for 25 minutes, until just set. Remove from the oven and cool on a rack for 10 minutes. Invert onto a sheet pan, remove the foil, and invert again on the rack to finish cooling. Cut carefully (the almonds will be harder to cut through than the brownie) with a serrated knife into 4 dozen bars.

The Dampest, Darkest, Deadliest Brownies of All Time

Brownies lend themselves to overstatement. I don't know how many brownie recipes I have seen (and titled myself) that are laden with superlatives. Allow me to add this one to your collection.

MAKES 16 LARGE BROWNIES

¹/₄ pound (1 stick) unsalted butter
4 ounces unsweetened chocolate, broken
  in pieces
1³/₄ cups dark brown sugar
Pinch of salt

2 teaspoons vanilla extract
3 eggs
1 cup flour
³/₄ cup semisweet chocolate chips

    Preheat oven to 375°F. Coat a 9-inch square baking pan with spray shortening.
    In a large, heavy-bottomed saucepan over medium heat, begin melting the butter. When it is half melted, add the chocolate. Remove from heat when the chocolate is half melted and stir until the butter and chocolate are completely melted.
    Stir in the sugar, salt, vanilla, and eggs until smooth. Stir in the flour until well combined. Mix in the chocolate chips.
    Pour and scrape the batter into the prepared pan. Bake for 23 minutes, until the top is dry but the center is still damp. Do not overbake. Remove from the oven and cool on a rack until the brownies are cool and firm, about 30 minutes. Cut into 16 squares.

Ugly Duckling Brownies

Don't let the leaden, crumbly look of these moist, rich brownies fool you. They are sensational: intensely chocolaty, exceptionally moist, and, yes, light as air.

MAKES 16 BROWNIES

4 tablespoons (¹/₂ stick) unsalted butter

5 ounces semisweet chocolate, broken in pieces

1 cup sugar

3 tablespoons cocoa powder

¹/₄ teaspoon salt

1 teaspoon vanilla extract

3 eggs

1 teaspoon baking powder

¹/₃ cup all-purpose flour

Preheat oven to 350°F. Coat a 9-inch square baking pan with spray shortening.

In a large, heavy-bottomed saucepan over medium heat, begin melting the butter. When it is half melted, add the chocolate. Remove from heat when the chocolate is half melted and stir until the butter and chocolate are completely melted.

Add the sugar, cocoa, salt, and vanilla, and stir until smooth. Beat in the eggs until completely incorporated. Add the baking powder in pinches to break up any lumps and stir thoroughly. Stir in the flour until well combined.

Pour and scrape the batter into the prepared pan. Bake for 25 to 30 minutes, until top is dry but a tester inserted in the center comes out with a damp crumb clinging to it. Do not overbake.

Remove the pan from the oven and cool on a rack for 30 minutes. Cut into 16 brownies and remove them with a small spatula. Don't be concerned if the first one out of the pan crumbles. These brownies are delicate and easily marred. Transfer the brownies to a cooling rack. Most of them will be fine, although they all will look a little ragged around the edges.

Marble Brownie Rounds

In these cupcake brownies, a bittersweet chocolate cake batter is swirled with milk chocolate. The lighter chocolate marbling comes from milk chocolate chips that naturally melt through the batter as the cupcakes bake.

MAKES 12 BROWNIES

¼ pound (1 stick) unsalted butter
3 ounces unsweetened chocolate, broken
  in pieces
1 teaspoon vanilla extract

1¼ cups sugar
3 eggs
1 cup flour
1 cup milk chocolate chips

Preheat oven to 350°F. Coat a 12-cup standard muffin tin with spray shortening.

In a large, heavy-bottomed saucepan over medium heat, begin melting the butter. When it is half melted, add the chocolate. Remove from heat when the chocolate is half melted and stir until the butter and chocolate are completely melted.

Stir in the vanilla, sugar, eggs, and flour until the batter is smooth. Stir in the chocolate chips.

Half-fill the cups of the muffin tin with the batter. Bake for 10 minutes, until firm but still soft in the center. Remove from the oven and cool on a rack for 10 minutes. Cover with plastic wrap and invert onto a sheet pan. Remove the pan and transfer brownies to a rack. Cool to room temperature.

Milk Chocolate Bars

These brownies are chewy and rich but not intensely chocolaty. Their pale mocha color classifies them as beigies.

MAKES 16 BEIGIES

$^1/_4$ **pound (1 stick) unsalted butter**
4 ounces milk chocolate, broken in pieces
1 cup sugar
$^1/_8$ **teaspoon salt**
1 teaspoon vanilla extract

2 tablespoons cream, light or heavy
2 eggs
1 cup flour
$^1/_2$ **cup milk chocolate chips**

Preheat oven to 350°F. Coat a 9-inch square baking pan with spray shortening.

In a large, heavy-bottomed saucepan over medium heat, begin melting the butter. When it is half melted, add the chocolate. Remove from heat when the chocolate is half melted and stir until the butter and chocolate are completely melted.

Stir in the sugar, salt, vanilla, cream, and eggs until the batter is smooth. Stir in the flour until well combined. Stir in the chocolate chips.

Pour and scrape the batter into the prepared pan and smooth the top. Bake for 25 minutes, until set but still soft in the center. Remove from the oven and cool until the pan can be touched. Cut into 16 pieces.

Pecan Butterscotch Beigies

Pralines—toasted pecans in caramelized sugar—were the inspiration for these sweet, chewy confections.

MAKES 16 BEIGIES

¹/₄ **pound (1 stick) unsalted butter**
³/₄ **cup pecan pieces**
1 **cup light brown sugar**
1 **teaspoon vanilla extract**
Pinch of salt

1 **egg**
1 **teaspoon baking powder**
1 **cup all-purpose flour**
1 **cup butterscotch morsels**

Preheat oven to 350°F. Coat a 9-inch square baking pan with spray shortening.

In a large, heavy-bottomed saucepan over medium heat, begin melting the butter. When it is half melted, add the pecan pieces and continue cooking until the pecans are lightly toasted. Remove from heat and stir in the sugar, vanilla, salt, and egg until smooth.

Add the baking powder in pinches to break up any lumps and stir thoroughly. Stir in the flour and mix until well combined. Stir in the butterscotch morsels.

Pour and scrape the batter into the prepared pan and spread into an even layer. Bake for 17 minutes, until lightly browned and just set. Remove from the oven and cool on a rack for 30 minutes. Cut into 16 pieces.

Almond Amaretto Blondies

These tortelike bar cookies are almond through and through. Use unpeeled almonds if you can. They will taste better and give these cookies an appealing, speckled appearance. Blanching, the method used to remove the brown, papery skin from almonds, leaves almonds attractively pale but tasting as if they had been steamed. If you can find only blanched ground almonds, improve their flavor by lightly toasting them in the butter before adding the sugar.

MAKES 16 BLONDIES

¹/₄ **pound (I stick) unsalted butter**	**Pinch of salt**
I ¹/₄ cups ground almonds	**I egg**
I cup sugar	**I teaspoon baking powder**
¹/₄ **teaspoon almond extract**	**I cup all-purpose flour**
2 tablespoons Amaretto	

Preheat oven to 350°F. Coat an 8-inch square baking pan with spray shortening.

In a large, heavy-bottomed saucepan over medium heat, begin melting the butter. When it is half melted, add the almonds and continue cooking, stirring constantly, until the butter is completely melted. Remove from heat and stir in the sugar, almond extract, Amaretto, salt, and egg until smooth. Add the baking powder in pinches to break up any lumps and stir thoroughly. Stir in the flour until well combined.

Pour and scrape the batter into the prepared pan and spread into an even layer. Bake for 20 minutes, until lightly browned and just set. Remove from the oven and cool on a rack for 30 minutes. Cut into 16 pieces.

Orange Praline Beigies

The combination of orange, brandy, pecans, and brown sugar gives these cookies a multidimensional flavor.

Makes 16 beigies

¹/₄ **pound (1 stick) unsalted butter**
1¹/₄ **cups ground pecans**
2 **teaspoons dried orange peel**
1 **cup light brown sugar**
¹/₂ **teaspoon vanilla extract**
¹/₄ **teaspoon orange extract**

2 **tablespoons brandy or liqueur,**
   preferably orange-flavored
Pinch of salt
1 **egg**
1 **teaspoon baking powder**
1 **cup all-purpose flour**

Preheat oven to 350°F. Coat an 8-inch square baking pan with spray shortening.

In a large, heavy-bottomed saucepan over medium heat, begin melting the butter. When it is half melted, add the pecans and orange peel and continue cooking, stirring constantly, until the butter is completely melted. Remove from heat and stir in the sugar, extracts, brandy or liqueur, salt, and egg until smooth. Add the baking powder in pinches to break up any lumps and stir thoroughly. Stir in the flour until well combined.

Pour and scrape the batter into the prepared pan and spread into an even layer. Bake for 20 minutes, until lightly browned and just set. Remove from the oven and cool on a rack for 30 minutes. Cut into 16 pieces.

Whole Wheat Blondies

These deceptively plain cookies have a decadent butterscotch flavor belying their nutrition-packed image.

MAKES 16 BLONDIES

¹/₄ **pound (1 stick) unsalted butter**
³/₄ **cup ground walnuts**
1 **cup light brown sugar**
1 **teaspoon vanilla extract**

Pinch of salt
1 **egg**
1 **teaspoon baking powder**
1 **cup whole wheat flour**

Preheat oven to 350°F. Coat a 9-inch square baking pan with spray shortening.

In a large, heavy-bottomed saucepan over medium heat, begin melting the butter. When it is half melted, add the walnuts and continue cooking until the nuts are lightly toasted. Remove from heat and stir in the sugar, vanilla, salt, and egg until smooth. Add the baking powder in pinches to break up any lumps and stir thoroughly. Stir in the flour until well combined.

Pour and scrape the batter into the prepared pan and spread into an even layer. Bake for 17 minutes, until lightly browned and just set. Remove from the oven and cool on a rack for 30 minutes. Cut into 16 pieces.

Fourth of July Brownies

Cranberries and blueberries in a white chocolate brownie batter give these bars their patriotic moniker. White chocolate is not chocolate at all, and it cooks differently from its darker namesake (see page 2). Keep the heat at medium, and make sure the white chocolate is almost completely melted before removing it from the stove.

MAKES 16 BROWNIES

4 tablespoons ($^1/_2$ stick) unsalted butter	3 eggs
4 ounces white chocolate chips	1 teaspoon baking powder
$^1/_2$ cup hazelnuts, finely chopped	6 tablespoons flour
$^3/_4$ cup sugar	$^1/_2$ cup dried cranberries
$^1/_8$ teaspoon salt	$^1/_2$ cup dried blueberries
1 teaspoon vanilla extract	$^3/_4$ cup mini–chocolate chips

Preheat oven to 350°F. Coat a 9-inch square baking pan with spray shortening.

In a large, heavy-bottomed saucepan over medium heat, begin melting the butter. When it is half melted, add the white chocolate chips. Remove from heat when the chocolate is nearly melted and stir until the butter and chocolate are completely melted.

Add the hazelnuts, sugar, salt, and vanilla, and stir until smooth. Beat in the eggs until completely incorporated. Add the baking powder in pinches to break up any lumps and stir thoroughly. Stir in the flour until the smooth batter forms. Stir in the cranberries, blueberries, and mini–chocolate chips until evenly distributed.

Pour and scrape the batter into the prepared pan and bake for 25 to 27 minutes, until the top is lightly browned and bounces back when pressed. Do not overbake.

Remove from the oven and cool on a rack for 30 minutes. Cut into 16 brownies and lift out with a small spatula.

One-Pot Cookies

Index